Existence

Existence

Christopher Manners

Poetica Press

First published in the USA
by Poetica Press 2019
an imprint of Sophia Perennis
© Christopher Manners 2018

For information, address:
Poetica Press, Ltd.
PO Box 253 El Prado, NM 87529
info@sophiaperennis.com

Paperback: 978-1-59731-182-3

Cover design: Michael Schrauzer

To my family

CONTENTS

Sacred Boyhood 1

In Pain 2

Youth Triumphant 4

Sorrow 7

Barbarians 9

Why? 10

Her Glory 12

The Lost Sword 13

This Human State 16

Golden Age 17

In Mourning 18

Punishment 20

Lost Joy 22

In Anguish 24

His Lament 25

To Revolt 26

Bellerophon 28

Rescued 30

At Sea 31

This Agonizing Abyss 33

Painful Emptiness 34

The Cage 36

Exile 37

The Fall of Youth 38

Bewildered 39

That Lady 40

In the Forest 41

Rebellion of the Giants 44

United with Sisyphus 48

Land of Pain 49

Despair 50

With a Seer 52

In Deep Sorrow 53

Struggling 54

The Knight 55

The Appearance 57

The Great Tempest 59

Pyrrhus and the Samnite 60

The Lake of Youth 63

The Solitary 64

Agony 66

Jupiter and Human Pain 67

The Venetian 68

Distant from her Eyes 71

The Hermit 72

Empedocles 74

Stunned 77

Warrior of the North 78

The Freedom of Youth 79

Polyphemus 80

Numa's Visitor 83

Profound Yearning 86

Her Glorious Eyes 87

Wrath 88

Cherished Meeting 91

In Misery 92

The Lament of Titus 93

Among all these Ruins 94

The Return 95

With Marcus Aurelius 97

Perplexed 98

The Warning of Tiresias 99

A Tuscan's Vision 100

The Centurion 102

In Battle 104

Towards Meaning 105

The Hermit's Address 106

Excruciating 107

Her Brilliant Eyes 108

The Wanderer 109

A Glimpse 111

Childhood Joy 112

The Longing Within 113

In the Cold 114

Striving at Sea 115

Tiberinus 116

Her Smile 118

In Milan 119

The Ego 122

The Ant Hill 123

In the North 124

Alexander in India 125

In the Desert 127

To be Free 128

Momentary Glance 129

In this Cave 130

Towards the Infinite 131

On the Path 132

Homesick 133

The Monk 134

Eternity Triumphant 137

A Knight 138

With Apollo 142

On the Wheel 144

Miraculous Eyes 145

The Sage of the Forest 146

To Unite 148

Sacred Boyhood

Always to treasure and hold,
I exalt my sacred boyhood youth,
that precious era gloriously bold,
closer to those stars of Truth;
venerating that exuberant time,
with those vibrant energies to keep,
it was a period miraculously sublime,
always to cherish in my soul deep.

With such abundant elation to maintain,
as a triumphant eagle in hopeful flight,
never any anguish then did stain,
while I soared to that stunning height.
Recalling now those earlier ways,
immersed in jubilation with friends dear,
nostalgia grows for those divine days,
when all was pure and peacefully clear,
as I was blessed with visions high,
conversing with those angels to revere,
yet my sudden fall I must decry,
left in these weary storms to steer.
All that prior glory so swiftly fled,
with this current desolation to deplore,
wandering miserably now as I tread,
and aching in my restless core.

But playing on those fields green,
I never felt the burden of the mind,
among those noble trees serene,
always those majestic delights to find.
To the highest skies the bliss did send,
riding with a valiant chariot's force,
as fleetingly I did wondrously ascend
to Eternity, to the Ultimate Source.

In Pain

As the glory of youth quickly flies,
losing those cherished joys prior,
now this existence I only despise,
left in this constant emptiness dire,
bombarded by this siege of anguish
through these long and barren years,
in this excruciating desert to languish,
consciousness torturing with its tears.

Without a grand meaning to find,
the vicious agony never does cease,
the vile void always plaguing my mind,
lacking the calm of precious peace,
immersed in this desolate abyss deep,
in this nothingness which does torment,
the pervasive lack causing me to weep,
churning in turmoil, this inner dissent.
And trapped in this war without end,
beleaguered by the relentless grief,
I'm forced now always to defend
against these invaders without relief,
as I must face the enemy in dismay,
with another grueling battle each day.

Always with this chasm to sense,
only futile everything does seem,
in my deepening despair immense,
as my perplexity continues to teem,
while fleeting joys inevitably fade,
those transient drops never enough,
as continual pain always does raid
amidst the harsh winds, always rough.

Wandering in these waters vast,
I'm battered by each mighty wave,
my hopes only diminishing fast,
now impossible my ship to save,
and I long from all this pain to flee,
while the void continues to grow,
so furious with this cruel sea,
as I sink into the darkness below.

Youth Triumphant

It was such a glorious time,
always with such jubilation high,
with boundless radiance sublime,
that wondrous joy as I did fly
in that precious garden pure,
with that flowing bliss to nourish,
and never any pain to endure
in ecstatic youth as I did flourish.

So with my valiant peers we did expand,
exploring with such a curious sense,
bravely venturing to many a distant land
with great ideals, vast dreams immense,
savouring the delights of our age of gold,
with ardent energies always to grow,
celebrating each majestic triumph bold,
while our endless hopes did always flow.

With Aeneas, to duty we were bound,
joining in our Latium, our sacred space,
sensing then the Absolute profound,
as we labored always with a clearer trace
of the pervading Divine which did resound,
building our city, as Romulus did found.
And soon our venerable Senate we did form,
and the elected Consuls took their place,
confident then to brave any storm,
with honour and fellowship to embrace.
Pursuing then many a noble mission,
our cherished Republic we did defend,
undaunted with each lofty ambition,

as our rising rapture did transcend.
With intimations of splendorous light,
we crafted those brilliant ideas of length,
amassing our legions of endless might,
bolstered by revered Scipio's strength,
as our arches and columns did stand,
always inspired by our purpose grand.

With the guiding eagle of Jupiter flying,
we were so passionate in our blessèd play,
with the owl of Minerva always smiling,
with never any moment of dismay.
Augmenting our frontiers with many a fort,
Mars always great fortitude did provide,
as any arrogant Catiline we would thwart,
our Republic thriving with more to reside,
and with such aspirations we did dwell,
as our seeking eyes did always beam,
as our beloved domain did swell,
while the limitless possibilities did teem.

So with such might I did surge,
rejoicing in the skies, freely to soar,
until those cruel invaders did emerge,
those ruthless barbarians to deplore,
those merciless hordes with their attack
leaving me in this desolation and lack.
So fleeting youth was destined to fall,
vanishing so sorrowfully as fading mist,
bringing such deep anguish to appall,
Time not permitting that joy to persist.

I lament that tragic loss with pain,
impossible in that euphoria to remain,
but to recall that blissful time Divine,
when I sensed many a higher sign,
briefly does uplift and console,
bringing some serenity to my mind,
while battling this aching inner hole,
with some deeper solace to find,
amidst the ruins which now surround,
venerating my sacred youth great,
as I recall that old triumphant sound
of my lost realm, my boyhood state.

Sorrow

All this sorrow through my years
has such profound depth and scope,
continually in these anguished tears,
as it diminishes my vital hope,
this aching emptiness so vast,
this misery which I cannot contain,
as I still struggle always downcast,
constantly battling this ruthless pain.

It is really boundless in its way,
as a great ocean endlessly deep,
this agony producing such dismay,
left in inescapable grief to weep,
in this turbulence which does torment,
my dwindling energies unable to keep,
as I'm driven now only to lament,
turning often to cherished sleep,
while this bitter fury does ferment,
with old ambitions unable to reap.
Imprisoned in this excruciating state,
as a sick bird unable even to fly,
I must question again my cold fate,
with the cosmos indifferent to my cry.

Disillusioned, I wander this sea,
its ravaging storms continually to fight,
never able these fierce winds to flee,
unable to muster that old might.
And towards the moon as I now gaze,
the troubling silence of the night
leaves me again in this bitter haze,
the solitude intensifying my plight,

tortured by the nothingness pervading,
still lost in this bewildering despair,
with this immense hole never fading,
and unable this descent to bear.

Yet with this cosmic pain I now feel
deeply connected to others in this way,
a higher bond which does appeal,
with this perplexing suffering each day.
Many are in this similar state to disdain,
united by this sorrow which does stir,
struggling here on this desolate plain,
and continuing the fight as we endure.

Barbarians

Why did the barbarians vile
suddenly so ruthlessly arrive?
Enduring now this harsh exile,
after that era when I did thrive,
that gloriously triumphant time,
immersed in youth's joy sublime.
But they brought such cruel fire,
invading with those hungry eyes,
leaving all these ruins dire,
all this destruction to despise,
and unable any longer to shield,
I lost my cherished command,
the barbarians never to yield,
bringing this anguish to my land.
My precious empire quickly did fall,
as only sorrow now does reign,
the depths of this abyss to appall,
plagued by this merciless pain;
trapped in this vicious torment,
and abandoned with my rage,
I was destined to lament,
now alone in this dark age.

Why?

"Why? Why?" is my endless cry,
through the restless and lonely night,
not content with illusory joys which fly,
as those wondrous birds of might,
which visited in childhood's height,
and no longer in their way return,
as my distress continues to churn,
still yearning for that clearer sight.
I'm not content with achievements here,
and all the vain goals we place ahead,
wandering uselessly as we steer,
only filled with increasing dread,
a dread which now brings this rage,
as we inevitably suffer and wane,
longing to escape this absurd stage,
and weary of this prison to disdain,
this wretched and torturing cage,
with the skies indifferent to our pain,
these skies which in their vastness alarm,
those cosmic reaches without end,
the continual silence which does disarm,
as in sinking nothingness I descend.

I must question this life's course,
the purpose of our struggling stay
in this land of desolation and dismay,
while agony pierces with its force.
The unknown continues to torment,
with all the tedium and toil to decry,
while the myriad meanings we invent
can never my aching core satisfy.
Climbing further, I must always endure

more sorrow on my arduous way,
as I can never gain that serenity pure,
but only more bewilderment each day,
still striving valiantly as I always seek,
yet there's never any fulfillment of mind,
and when I reach another high peak
only more plaguing emptiness then I find,
so vicious as it returns again to tear,
this encompassing abyss immense,
constantly battling this anguished sense,
the underlying turmoil always there.

Her Glory

When upon her glory I first did gaze,
upon her radiance in its emanating way,
I flew suddenly into that deepening haze,
so utterly enchanted on that fateful day,
and encountering those illuminating rays,
completely under her stunning sway,
I briefly escaped the chained maze,
no longer in that suffering dismay,
as momentously I then did realize
that majestic Beauty was truly Divine,
longing forever to behold those eyes,
from Eternity a wondrous sign.

The Lost Sword

At a temple, a young Roman chosen by fate
received a sudden vision, fleeting but of force,
seeing the mountains of the North great,
the wondrous sight racing as a horse;
deeply compelled to this spot to advance,
he quickly began on his course ahead,
as this vision did so swiftly entrance,
unsure of its meaning, but ready to tread.

During the Roman's trek, Mars then did appear,
walking along his path and approaching near.
"For your piety, much favour you have gained,
as it was decided that I should now emerge,
as much blood has already the land stained,
while a pivotal battle is now on the verge.
As you have honoured the sacred tradition,
you are now tasked with a glorious mission:
with valor, you will proceed without fear
and travel to the Alps to critically retrieve
the lost sword of Romulus, my son dear,
stolen by the Gauls, a cause to grieve.
I shall provide the sword's resting place,
your destiny to recover amid the snow,
as the cruel Carthaginians we now face,
that grueling war still continuing to flow,
and to Scipio you will provide with grace,
as his valiant army's strength will grow,
inspiring the troops with the sword's sight
in those hours before Zama's crucial fight.
A momentous victory Rome will then attain,
as its dominant power must then expand,
with supremacy in the Mediterranean to gain,
venturing ahead to new and distant land."

"But why have the gods of the sky
chosen me for this task so high,
especially with my illness in its way,
weakening my strength each weary day?
Though honoured and to my duty bound,
a stronger man surely can be found."

"You must not doubt your capacity bold,
as your role we already did ordain,
recognizing your tenacity through the cold,
with immortal honour now to obtain."

"But I must inquire now, as you are here:
why is this life filled with pain so grave,
continually dominated by war, so many a tear,
with so many afflictions always to brave?
For lasting tranquility I so deeply yearn,
yet there's always another battle to be fought,
not only against our barbaric enemies to spurn,
in inevitable lines of combat always caught,
but against illness, against sorrow and grief,
always such suffering in this woeful life brief."

"That deep serenity you will not find
until wondrous Elysium you finally reach,
while life here is certainly of a troubled kind,
with deep suffering, the experience of each.
Yet it is necessary, as only Jupiter does know,
for you to struggle while this pain does flow,
climbing with honour, labouring to thrive,
battling all that agony towards the height,
with your purpose continuing to strive,
as you develop deeper that radiant might."
Leaving him in thought, now Mars did depart,
the Roman with assurance in his inspired heart.

So he proceeded with strength and zeal,
even amidst all his affliction's pain,
to the mountain which Mars did reveal,
moving ardently through the plain.
The fierce wind a hindrance on his path,
he climbed now the massive peak,
struggling through the winter's wrath,
continuing through his ache to seek,
even as the snow obscured his view,
even as his burning doubts still grew.
So always with duty in his steady mind,
ready with all his devotion to discover,
sensing the grand significance of the find,
finally the sword he was grateful to uncover,
in reverent awe that it once did belong
to the great founder, filled with such pride,
rejoicing then in his jubilant song,
on his triumphant chariot to ride.

So proceeding to a Ligurian port,
he was ready on the sea to commence,
sensing that Neptune himself did escort
his passage through the waves immense;
he reflected on the war, its raging harm,
the devastating battles with death vast,
the engulfing struggle which did so alarm,
yet he knew Rome's brilliance, meant to last.
Soon he was grateful to arrive on land,
towards the Roman camp as he did progress,
rushing ahead, with his pain to withstand,
always fighting his plaguing distress.
So with Scipio considering his strategy's design,
finally the delivery he was joyous to complete,
the general holding the sword, a day divine,
with intimations of destiny as they did meet.

This Human State

Into this arduous existence thrown,
with a lack of understanding and reason,
with the underlying purpose unknown,
I'm struggling through this lonely season,
the meaningless vacuum bringing pain,
while the aching toil seems only vain.
With the threat of nothingness to face,
and piercing sorrow to withstand,
I must question this weary chase,
forced to traverse this perplexing land,
always coping with emptiness immense
and the terror of this nihilistic sense;
gazing at the grey of the silent sky,
as the distress continues to brew,
this restless ennui I must decry,
never knowing which path to pursue.
Always in this furious abyss of fear,
I sail tediously in this harsh sea,
tired of this tragic farce unclear,
never able from this dread to flee,
and the angst now induces a tear,
while I yearn so deeply to finally hear
the true purpose of this vile life,
the enigma still torturing as I steer,
amid this recurring storm of strife,
the constant suffering always near.

Golden Age

It was a wondrous era of jubilant height,
with rising hopes and ideals great,
of vibrant energy and boundless might,
blessed with bliss in that sacred state.
During those playful days sublime,
in those serene fields, always pure,
childhood was such a golden time,
with never any suffering to endure.

Running with euphoria profound,
I was connected to the Infinite High,
as the trumpets in glory would resound,
as a brilliant eagle in elation to fly;
in the splendor of Arcadia I did roam,
never with any restless tedium or pain,
among the shepherds in my idyllic home,
always content during Saturn's reign,
completely unburdened and free to soar,
with never any sense of the futile or vain,
always aspiring in harmony to explore,
back in those cherished days to adore.

I never thought the joy would cease,
the birds always in song in that life,
enjoying those calm waters of peace,
not yet aware of existence's strife.
But it was fated too swiftly to end,
from that summit to so painfully fall,
and into vast sorrow I did descend,
into this desert which does appall.
For that lost joy I now keenly yearn,
before the corruption and decline,
homesick and longing to return
to that radiant jubilation Divine.

In Mourning

She is an astounding Lady sublime,
with the ideal perfection of her face,
but I can only mourn at this time,
always so elusive with her pace.
I remember when I first did see
her miraculous beauty so high,
briefly out of the cave and free
as an eagle soaring in the sky,
as she calmed my ravaging storm,
to wondrous new heights to fly,
as the experience did transform,
quickly rescued from my desert dry.
I was shocked to see her light,
gifted with an ecstatic vision Divine,
upon that stunning celestial sight,
as victorious Love did suddenly shine,
with those chariots jubilantly profound,
seeing many a grand temple and shrine,
as all those trumpets did so resound,
closer to the Supreme Infinite to align.

Still reeling from those glorious eyes,
and that smile which did astound,
with such grief I painfully did realize
that she was already with another bound,
crippled then by a dreadful lance,
as I recognized that I lacked the chance
with her in cherished Love to ever unite,
as the agony of war is now so fierce,
destined this invading anguish to fight,
as the desolation still does pierce.
Abandoned in this solitude as I weep,

she will never return my Love,
sinking swiftly into this ocean deep,
always questioning the Realm Above;
I saw those eyes which did transcend,
yet now this vast sorrow does ensnare,
from boundless heights only to descend
into this lamentation and despair.

Punishment

A punishment human existence does seem,
after a primordial transgression lost to time,
as such anguish and despair does teem,
with only fleeting glimpses of the sublime.
With all the excessive torture and turmoil,
these harsh afflictions which never cease,
with all the despondent and dreary toil,
it's impossible to secure any peace,
as consciousness continues to torment,
always questioning this perplexing descent.

With some enigmatic and sinful stain,
some cruel decision we cannot comprehend,
we seem exiled from our previous domain,
to this miserable world to quickly descend,
with Jupiter thundering from the remote sky,
banished from a prior glory once so high,
utterly astounded by our wretched fate,
sent away to this distant land to scorn,
enduring the mystery of our aching state,
always in this agonizing abyss to mourn.

Imprisoned in this body, in this life mundane,
always with this angst and ennui to dread,
I struggle with the weight of each chain,
through these battles, still marching ahead.
With all our suffering on this corrupt plane,
I move tediously through each storm,
as everything is only lacking and vain,
without the splendor of our original form,

and unable the meaning to understand,
without that sweet freedom to fly,
my tearful questions always expand,
still trapped in this desert dry.

Lost Joy

As a bird soaring in wondrous flight,
each triumph of joy did so resound
in that jubilant era of Augustan height,
in those old days of elation profound.
With all those aspirations of length,
when that stunning bliss I did find,
I held that boundless energy of strength,
before any woes would plague the mind,
as I commanded such an inspiring fleet,
through the distant waves to explore,
always with new possibilities to greet,
venturing ardently to every shore.
All those marble structures I did raise,
temples with blessed columns high,
and all those thriving cities to praise,
flourishing with the gods of the sky.

Yet from that glory I've been banished
and all that splendor has been lost,
as cherished Juventas has vanished,
her shrine in wretched ruins in the frost,
and my marching legions once proud,
which were once invincible in might
have only departed as a fading cloud,
leaving me solitary in this aching night.
Consciousness was different in that land,
when that joy did astonishingly flow,
before my awareness did then expand,
before this void did agonizingly grow.

As valiant Belisarius the Goths did fight,
recovering lost land, with the menacing sight
of those savage intruders without end,

I struggle now my endless pains to mend.
And I search for some implausible way
for renewal amidst all this deep dismay,
yet already fallen is my empire great,
my formidable despair never to abate.
Unable that magnificence to retrieve,
I'm left to suffer through this fate,
as for youth's end I can only grieve,
declining in my anguished state.

In Anguish

Always with anguish to withstand,
beauty and joy are fleetingly short
in the vast desolation of this land,
harshly exiled from that old court
into the corrupt misery of this place,
amidst all this strife throughout,
with these fears and floods to face,
with each pestilence and drought;
and trapped in this senseless race,
the sick with their cries still shout,
those cries which seem unheard,
as precious serenity we're without,
while I observe many a dying bird,
despair always reigning with its clout.
And emptiness resurfaces in its way,
as a ruthless creature from below,
tormenting as the tempests grow,
with these lonely winds of dismay.
Lacking calm and cherished peace,
I'm never fulfilled in this vicious cold,
as endless ambitions only increase,
and excessive suffering I behold
in this grueling trial of length,
under the enigmatic sky still grey,
losing youth's transient strength,
and baffled each restless day.

His Lament

Engulfed by this constant strife,
continuing to question His Design,
I must protest against this painful life,
always perplexed by the Divine.
Does God in his way really care
for each individual on this harsh soil,
as we're flooded with such despair,
aching in this land of suffering and toil?

Abandoned in this life which I scorn,
I peer at all the stars from my small boat,
condemned now to struggle and mourn,
while God is still inscrutable and remote;
with this excruciating pain in my core,
with no apparent meaning to secure,
through all these lonely days to deplore,
this existence I can barely endure.

To Revolt

In this anguished existence of pain,
deeply weary of each distressing day,
I'm compelled now to rise in my way
against all the suffering on this plain,
to revolt against the low gods cruel,
against the flawed demiurge old,
as volcanic rage continues to fuel
my erupting fury intrepidly bold.

Ready to storm the Olympian height,
as valiant Otus and Ephialtes did dare,
to join with the Giants of ancient might,
always trapped in our desolate despair,
gathering more men in an uprising great,
the merciless tyrant on his throne to reach,
weary of the punitive workings of fate,
yet we shall strive now to finally breach,
aspiring with our tenacity to overthrow,
with a great siege of their selfish lair,
no longer permitting the floods to flow,
no longer with this misery to bear.
With audacious Prometheus to inspire,
sympathetic to humanity's condition,
with his heroic theft of the illuminating fire,
he emboldens us on our noble mission,
that glorious Titan to always revere,
strengthening us as we now commence,
augmenting our forces without fear,
ready to climb to that peak immense.

I must rebel against this arduous life,
as the boundless agony doesn't relent,
immersed in this ache of endless strife,

in this tragic prison to always resent,
in this flawed, grieving world to disdain,
forced all this suffering to withstand,
always on this stormy journey vain,
and condemned to this forsaken land.
With all the vast emptiness forlorn,
the torturing void never to cease,
this mode of consciousness I scorn,
searching the seas for elusive peace.
Too much pain here does pervade,
as excruciating illness plagues the mind,
destined so quickly to decay and fade,
with all this distress which does bind,
and the gods only indifferent seem,
as the cosmos never seems to care,
while all our woes constantly teem,
while at these skies I continually stare.

Bellerophon

"Why are you in this lowly state grey,
as woefully mournful you now appear?
Are you not Bellerophon, adored and dear,
who the vicious Chimaera once did slay?"
He had found him despondent in a cave,
ailing in his diminished condition grave.

"Yes I am Bellerophon once great,
but now in misery I only lament,
in this dire agony, mourning my fate,
trapped always in this aching torment.
I once flew with Pegasus through the air,
but the gods are so cruel in their way,
leaving me now in this barren despair,
still churning in my furious dismay.
The fierce Chimaera I did meet,
fulfilling the prophecy of an old sage,
so proud to finally conquer and defeat
that formidable beast of such rage,
and I faced then many an additional foe,
audaciously engaging without fear,
stubborn enemies attempting to grow,
as so many challengers I did subdue,
with glorious victories always near,
as radiant honours I then did gain,
with more might to swiftly accrue,
as I was recognized through the plain.

But then burning with my endless desire,
I longed so vigorously for divine power,
unable to appease my boundless fire,
deciding to soar to the gods' realm high,

boldly ascending at that critical hour,
until cruel Zeus sent that stinging fly,
and then back to Earth I did suddenly fall,
left forsaken in this state which does appall.

I've wandered for years in my grief,
contemplating this life, so limited and brief.
To join the gods was my desire deep,
not satisfied with this tiring world mundane,
this pitiful existence where we often weep,
which so intensely I must disdain.
Sent here to suffer through the long night,
only for my inevitable end I now wait,
always with another vile creature to fight,
so disillusioned by our wretched state.
And though I lament my lost glory bold,
I see now my past labours as only vain,
with nothing in this ruthless life to hold,
and nothing really meaningful to gain,
while the remote gods now I only scorn,
as we're ants, insignificant as we cry,
left perplexed, so furiously forlorn,
always lonely and soon to die."

Rescued

When into her glorious eyes I did gaze,
my very existence she did transform,
such a joyous rescue from desolate days,
after struggling through that dreadful storm.
After wandering in that desert to decry,
I was shocked as her light did appear,
so astounded by the way she did fly,
always to cherish those eyes so dear,
and as her stunning smile I did behold,
I was blessed with energies immense,
finally escaping that weary prison old,
and revitalized with a wondrous sense
of the Divine Love which does reign,
with triumphant hope in my ardent soul,
aware of the splendor of the higher plane,
no longer plagued by that restless hole,
as I was rejuvenated in my battered core,
her miraculous beauty to always inspire,
finally able with sweet freedom to soar,
with renewed trust in the Infinite Higher.

At Sea

In the struggle with Carthage, the enemy old,
while many encounters on the waves did flow,
before audacious Hannibal's crossing bold,
with the Punic threat continuing to grow,
a Roman captain was now in much dismay,
under the command of Regulus, his valiant name,
attempting to return to the fleet, making his way,
as the Carthaginian menace they aspired to tame.
After the victory at Ecnomus, that clash of force,
he was battered by storms, taken off his course,
as ominous winds pushed him for many a day,
targeted by the gods and suddenly thrown,
his vessel tossed and swiftly blown astray,
separated from the fleet and perilously alone.

Still reeling from the storm which did amaze,
the captain now noticed a ship in the haze,
deciding the strange vessel now to approach,
his crew in agreement, not providing reproach,
and so they made the encounter without fear,
as an enemy craft it did not appear,
and soon the two ships did promptly meet,
as a solitary man did emerge to greet.

So this sailor the captain began to question,
as the old man his past began to reveal,
with his weary and beleaguered expression,
his unique misery which they quickly did feel.
"Back in my daring youth, never meek,
I vigorously explored and did curiously seek
the secrets of the gods, understanding divine,

questing for higher answers, for many a sign.
In Rome during its infancy I began my life,
before Brutus expelled that last King in strife,
but despite warnings as my father did beseech,
through my search I did eagerly overreach.
Tired of the priests, with each elaborate rite,
I sought hidden knowledge with such desire,
with my ravenous vanity of selfish might,
and my hunger growing as voracious fire.

So eventually I provoked Jupiter's wrath,
no longer able to tolerate my zealous path,
and he turned to Neptune who did allocate
my vicious punishment, determining my fate,
and so I was condemned with great disdain
to wander these seas perpetually in pain.
So to precious land I can never return,
plagued by my despair without relief,
tormented by all this emptiness as I burn,
as I wander these seas in my lonely grief."

This Agonizing Abyss

I'm dying now in this barren cold,
in this relentless blizzard of pain,
lacking a reliable foundation to hold,
as all my efforts are merely vain,
enduring a dreaded attack each day,
my precious kingdom unable to defend,
while the enemy continues to send
my weary mind into deeper dismay.
Harshly abandoned and always alone,
I continue to fight with a battered core,
tortured by this tempestuous unknown,
and remote from that treasured shore,
sinking into these depths now as I fade
into this agonizing abyss so deep,
as nothingness continues to pervade,
left in this darkness only to weep.

Painful Emptiness

Tied to existence, there's inherent pain,
a pervading emptiness always deep,
inevitably emerging on this plain,
and compelling so many to weep.
Though with many aspirations I yearn,
each anguished day does torment,
while my cherished city still does burn,
the ruthless invaders never to relent,
constantly forced to defend and fight
for my beleaguered kingdom once-great,
yet destroyed is my dear castle of might,
always questioning the cruelty of fate,
and this horrid plague has yet to subside,
all destined so quickly to decay and die,
as this wretched life I can only deride,
hearing the sick children as they cry.
Continually besieged on this bleak soil,
such useless vanity I always sense,
condemned to this exhausting toil,
and trapped in this agony immense.

Devastated by this unfulfilled desire,
excruciating as an enemy lance,
I must always face this crippling fire,
wandering in this miserable trance;
then torturing ennui brings its fleet,
mercilessly attacking in its way,
impossible such strength to defeat,
leaving me in my grieving dismay.
This emptiness, a menacing scourge,
sinking deeper into my despair,
has brought me to the raging verge

of hopelessness, unable to bear.
And though for the heights I still aim,
is the climb even meaningful as I seek?
Unable all this furious pain to tame,
I expect only more emptiness at the peak.

The Cage

With this vast boredom to bear,
in agitation through the entire day,
at the perplexing sky I now stare,
as I question the necessity of my stay
in this empty desert to deplore,
while I'm unable any sleep to gain,
so distant from that golden shore,
while all these endless queries remain.
And in this torturous land, only forlorn,
with each cruel illness and decline,
with the inevitability of sorrow's chain,
tired of that meager, fleeting shine,
this intolerable enigma I must scorn,
always wistful for that prior age,
while this ennui continues to confine,
with this world only a miserable cage,
in this wretched condition to mourn,
as in this weariness I only wane,
wounded permanently and torn,
and longing to escape all the pain.

Exile

Why was I exiled to this agonizing land,
with tormenting consciousness to bear,
with this relentless angst, unable to stand,
trapped in this desolate chasm of despair?
Why was I sent to this barren plain,
with these despised afflictions severe,
always with these burdens to sustain,
while merciless plagues strike with fear,
through all these empty days to disdain,
famine unceasing through the years,
with all this exhausting toil vain,
in this wretched land of endless tears?
I know that it was glorious before,
with blissful joy and peace serene,
yet now this aching lack I must deplore
in these darkened fields never green.
In this wilderness of devastating cold,
why did I have to take this human form,
always battling for strength to hold,
and forced to endure each weary storm?

The Fall of Youth

Fallen is my cherished empire,
as I still mourn in sinking dismay,
recalling all the vile rage and fire
of the vicious barbarians on that day,
when my realm of joy they did attack
with their ruthless hunger savage,
leaving me now in this despairing lack,
as my precious capital they did ravage.
It was once so jubilant as I did thrive,
flourishing with all those wonders vast,
until those cruel invaders did then arrive,
with all my elation not meant to last,
as that dire destruction they did spread,
now only sensing this dreary decay,
as that cherished eagle so quickly fled,
while suddenly I lost each vibrant ray.
And as these weary ruins surround,
considering this collapse of woe,
with broken columns on the ground,
only deep anguish now does grow,
as I'm left with emptiness profound,
as the flooding tears endlessly flow
in this grief as I can't comprehend
the swiftness of my devastating fall,
reigning fleetingly only to descend
into this agony which does appall.

Bewildered

As this pain and sorrow does converge,
though I believe in God Supreme,
these nihilistic thoughts now emerge,
as so bewildering it all does seem.
What's the reason for being here,
in this desolate, unsatisfying way,
as deep agony is always so near,
with suffering's devastating sway?
Are we meant in some way to advance,
the soul developing through these tears,
while facing each long earthly trance,
gaining wisdom through all the years,
the struggling soul growing as we mend,
overcoming hardships and despair,
labouring to know and to transcend,
and purifying for the serene air?

Were we free to avoid the descent
into this barren material world to bewail,
where the storm never does relent,
always through such furious winds to sail?
And is it our duty this voyage to endure,
on this tempestuous and aching course,
before we reach that High Realm pure,
before we return, closer to the Source?
As a tiny species in the lonely cosmos vast,
is the Infinite indifferent to the human race,
our fleeting triumphs not destined to last,
toiling towards these futile goals to chase?
This life still meaningless does seem,
as only painful emptiness I now embrace,
as excessive affliction does teem,
through this vast nothingness to face.

That Lady

Her face did completely astound,
leaving me utterly entranced for days,
shocked that such beauty could be found,
as I was drifting in that deepening haze.
Completely captivated by her glory high,
stunned by such splendor to meet,
to new heights she propelled me to fly,
not prepared for such eminence to greet.
And as her miraculous eyes did glow,
there was that sudden emanating light,
which so mysteriously continued to flow,
as I was immobilized and lacking might,
with such unrivalled perfection to behold,
while her radiance so quickly did blind,
as she was surely of that higher mold,
humbled by such a goddess to find.

But never would I be blessed to gain
another occasion her brilliance to see,
as the ensuing sorrow I did disdain,
longing from this cruel world to flee.
Another unattainable Lady to produce
more misery and ongoing lament,
her disappearance then did reduce
my life to grief, to piercing torment,
sinking in that endless ocean deep,
with that loss of a glorious chance,
recalling that painful last glance,
left in that devastation to weep.

In the Forest

In this lonely forest of dread,
amidst these weary trees dark,
those old certainties have fled,
as this sorrow continues to mark
my remote path as I tread,
searching for a deeper spark.
Wandering in my long despair
and yearning for a sacred beam,
I'm sinking in this pain; yet where
is God, the Absolute Supreme?

Even with my great longing deep,
it is so arduous on this course
to know God, the Ultimate Source,
abandoned here as I often weep
in this forsaken and deserted land,
in the ruthless cold as I only freeze,
losing those old aspirations grand,
always lacking that tranquil breeze.
I hope for a joyous and loving embrace,
yet fear that the enigmatic Infinite may,
with all this strife and agony we face,
be only remote in its unfathomable way,
as we're merely these vain ants small,
amid the immensity which does appall.
And in this desolate place, always far,
cherished birds no longer resound,
tending to every wound and scar,
as the empty silence does surround
and now I wonder how to last

as my solitude does torment,
insignificant in this cosmos vast,
and bewildered as I must lament.

Where are the sages to revere,
the venerable hermits of old,
all the adored seers so dear,
who once the mysteries did behold?
With their probing, illuminated eyes,
the ancients did wondrously provide
that deeper understanding wise,
with wayward travellers to guide,
with glorious wisdom to console,
assisting with that aching hole.
Yet I only seem now to meet
those who their proud egos raise,
blindly holding their self complete,
and forgetting the Infinite to praise.
O Europa, sons of Athens and Rome,
what over the years did transpire?
You once recognized your true home,
the splendor of the Realm Higher;
and abundant with those of sight,
you once the dear Infinite knew,
seeking that jubilant height,
those devoted souls which flew.

I'm still in this forest with thought,
with this plaguing pain caught,
yet surely this anguished sense
of distant separation intense
is really only an illusion mere,

as I must relinquish all my fear,
as the pure soul is always allied
to the Source and eternally tied.
And being truly Infinite in kind,
its Goodness must be without end,
so this Source and Supreme Mind,
to which we all aspire to ascend,
must for its creation love and care,
providing the opportunity to find
for souls which strive to be aligned,
to reach the glory of the celestial air.
Always aching and unfulfilled without,
now towards unity so deeply I yearn,
after braving each distressing drought,
as to boundless Eternity I must return.

Rebellion of the Giants

Back in those ancient and perilous days,
when humans with the Giants did co-exist,
the numerous Giants of formidable ways,
emerging with valor from their lairs of mist,
with their raging rulers swiftly became
envious of the gods' power, to deeply despise,
plotting their overthrow, a proud war to proclaim,
as soon with great fervor the Giants did rise,
rallying together from every distant land,
so zealously hungry to gain command.

Soon the warfare did ensue, intense in scope,
and the Giants with their audacious hope
soon to humanity then did eagerly request
assistance in the combat, which did test
the Giants' resolve, their courage and strength,
in this massive struggle of grueling length.
And tempting the humans to join the fight,
they offered a notable place in the new regime,
with vulnerable humanity appalled in fright,
and the Giants appealing to many a dream,
as they reminded men of their afflicted life,
with Zeus indifferent to each lamenting cry,
with all the arduous toil and grief so rife,
and their mortal nature so fleetingly to fly.
Thus humanity soon joined the Giants' side,
arming the daring rebels with more supply,
and a great mass of troops they did provide,
as the Giants then bombarded the sky.

Massive boulders the Giants did throw,
and all these immense trees aflame,

as their confidence continued to grow,
as with their enraged efforts they did claim
the end of Olympian rule, long unjust,
each Giant seeking individual fame,
with Zeus' cruel authority never to trust,
towards his dwelling itself to aim.
Soon some of the gods did descend
to fight the resilient Giants on their soil,
surprised by all the fury which did extend
and all the assisting humans disloyal.
A momentous revolt against Zeus' reign,
the Giants were unyielding on their path,
as these daring warriors did seem
unstoppable in their determined wrath,
and then continuing with such sheer force,
they began on a new and ambitious course,
piling great mountains to reach and invade,
the realm of the gods itself so high,
in an unprecedented and fearless raid,
as they voraciously did anticipate and eye
the sweetness of expected victory ahead,
no longer in that subservience to dread.

Engulfing chaos the war did create,
as proud Zeus then on Hercules did call,
the hero skillfully shooting his arrows of fate,
bringing down many Giants, as they did fall.
But even with intrepid Hercules at their side,
the gods still couldn't end the rebellion brave,
and with such ferocity the Giants did stride
ardently towards the palace as they did crave.

Then Zeus himself was ready to join the fight,
using his thunderbolts of power renowned,
unleashing such tremendous might,
and intervening with that roaring sound;
even ruthless Zeus eventually did tire,
the earth so devastated by raging fire,
yet he mustered more energies immense,
ready once again the insurgents to meet,
resuming his striking onslaught in defense,
as his remaining foes he finally did defeat,
the revolt finally crushed that fateful night,
with Zeus returning to his majestic seat,
the gods celebrating in their jubilant height,
as the threat they did so crucially expel,
decisively clearing that alarming blight,
while the Giants to their harsh deaths fell.

So after such long fighting and gore,
Zeus became more tyrannical in his rule,
solidifying his power, his order to restore,
and with his subordinates much more cruel.
Now asserting his dominant control,
he was furious in realizing humanity's role,
allied to the vanquished Giants savage,
which he had been so satisfied to ravage,
and vengeful action then Zeus did intend,
his intense punishment so swiftly to send.

So then with this matter to address,
he quickly and harshly did decide
that humanity would face more distress,
as their recent efforts he did so deride,
condemning humans in their disgrace

to much deeper suffering then to face,
with even more consciousness self-aware,
with more sensitivity and emotional pain,
that mental anguish often to ensnare,
much different than the days of the past,
always difficult to endure and sustain
all this sorrow and agony vast.

United with Sisyphus

I'm united with Sisyphus old,
condemned in this miserable way,
punished for forgotten sins bold,
and left in our anguished dismay.
Up that wretched hill again in disdain,
forced to roll the boulder ahead,
we're crippled by this mournful pain,
always with this endless toil to dread,
immersed in our boundless woe,
impossible to escape this agony great,
our piercing sorrow always to flow,
questioning again mysterious fate.
Plagued by the torturous strife,
I sense all the vast futility vain,
the nothingness of this useless life,
the emptiness of this tearful plain,
with this desolation to so appall,
and the horrid insignificance of all.
And on this hill we often converse,
prisoners in this unbearable condition,
furious as we're forced to traverse,
questioning the purpose of this mission,
fighting the boredom as we discourse,
enduring together this excruciating state,
exhausted by this senseless course,
and united in all our grief to relate.
And we're weary of this cruel torment,
descending further into misery deep,
as meaningless life we only resent,
in this shared darkness as we weep.

Land of Pain

Why am I here, in this lowly land of pain,
in this world of such grief and turmoil,
where every invented meaning is vain,
always with such futility and toil?
Forced to march, with weary labour,
what is there in existence to really attain,
while our fragile health only does waver,
with this constant suffering to sustain?

Burdened by the need to achieve higher,
and never truly fulfilled in any way,
with infinite ambitions, always to aspire,
I'm trapped in this despair each day,
while we're so lacking in vanishing time
for all our hopes, each aspiration bold,
as I search for the fleeting sublime,
with old dreams so difficult to hold.
And with all of tedium's growing strife,
with boredom's crippling weight,
I'm infuriated by this miserable life,
unable to fathom this sinking state.

Lamenting the loss of that youthful fort,
my energies are only fading as I steer
through decaying life, empty and short,
with death always looming so near.
And as this flood continues to teem,
I yearn no longer to be bound,
as that departure now does seem
a welcome liberation to resound.

Despair

"I'm laboring through all this tedious toil,
coping with this deep sorrow and pain,
while harsh fate always seems to foil
those old hopes I once did maintain,
as this dissatisfaction always does lurk
in this existence which I so disdain,
tired of all this exhausting work,
while I lack a purpose on this plain.
So as inevitable death does await,
rendering it all futile, and value without,
I'm so weary of this unbearable state,
always trapped in this devastating drought.
So as there seems no meaning to derive,
why in this life should I even survive?"

"But my friend, know that you are meant to fly,
and recall your duty to God, to the Infinite High."

"But what duty? In this land of suffering unjust,
where children to absurd illness lose their life,
where so many struggle amid the cruel strife,
to continue this questioning now I must.
God's existence we're not able to know,
with nothing definitive now to embrace,
as the daily agony continues to flow,
battling this anguish which I always face.
But what does He need? Why did He create?
Why do we matter to Him, in our pitiful state?"

"I see that many questions plague your mind,
burdened as Atlas with oppressing weight,
but God provided us with the freedom great

to strive to seek His everlasting Love and find,
with the freedom of a purpose here to discover,
as we strive ultimately His glory to uncover.
But your crucial faith you must always hold
in God, and the striving soul to maintain,
in cherished immortality and meaning bold,
with this existence truly not in vain."

"Yet the lack of certainty I lament,
as this unknown we have to endure,
as death with its mystery does torment,
with the aching sorrow always to recur.
I don't like His plan, this creation of tears,
forced to suffer through the miserable years.
So as the great Prometheus chained,
without any lasting solace to be found,
my rage can no longer be contained,
my fury against this existence to abound.
Difficult to tame this wrath immense,
existence is just too painful as I declare,
with only meaningless days to sense,
always crippled by this despair."

With a Seer

"With my proud legion, I did send
my men into fierce battle many a time,
as we with valiant honour did defend
the greatness of Rome, her glory sublime.
After serving many posts over the years,
I've observed so often the cruel stain
of agonizing suffering and all the tears,
which pervade this life of endless pain.
So I come to you friend in perplexity great,
once again for your wise words to hear,
troubled by all this grief assigned by fate,
these continuous woes always near."

"This pain will lead you soon to purify
those inner waters as you uncloud
your immortal core of boundless light,
no longer with your attachments proud,
advancing to greater planes as you fly,
on that voyage to the One to unite.
Many lives in this land we must endure,
persisting with honour and noble might,
even as all the sorrow continues to stir,
striving to soar to that liberating sight,
to finally reach that cleansed state pure,
as we yearn for that blissful height."

In Deep Sorrow

In deep sorrow, struggling with many a tear,
gazing at the stars in this despairing state,
I'm reminded of boyhood days so dear,
before this prison, this crippling weight.
Nostalgic for the wonder of that elated time,
it was a peaceful reign, so jubilantly free,
as there was such abundant joy sublime,
roaming with shepherds, visiting the sea,
with such tranquil purity in that age,
before the inevitable corruption to lament,
which would only usher in a new stage
of familiar sorrow since that descent;
those invaders poured onto the plain,
prompting that relentless combat grave,
my exhausted legions unable to sustain,
my cherished empire impossible to save,
as those cruel new forces did emerge,
quickly tormenting my beleaguered mind,
as anguish and rage then did merge,
that old serenity never again to find.
Weeping as I recall my days pure,
I must now question God's plan higher,
as this excessive pain we must endure,
sent swiftly into this desolation dire,
and even as we climb and nobly aspire,
our joy is then only fleetingly brief,
as these tedious days constantly tire,
always mourning in my endless grief.

Struggling

Struggling with my tortured mind,
mourning endlessly in this torment,
I can't bear this isolation confined,
left in my bitter loneliness to lament,
enduring my days in this dreary cell,
as I still contemplate that descent,
amidst all my sorrows which swell,
swiftly to this vicious prison sent.
And as I continue now to reflect,
the nature of existence I must scold,
with only misery and tedium to detect,
deserted in this cruel abyss cold,
the ruthless agony attacking each day,
losing my vigorous energies old,
long trapped in excruciating dismay,
with my hopes impossible to hold.

The Knight

A bold knight much distance did traverse,
through the dense forests on his path,
towards a remote hermit to converse,
now weary of life and growing in wrath,
as such grief and perplexity he did face,
trapped with all his disillusioned dismay,
but new hopes on this chance he did place,
towards the hermitage as he made his way.

Perceiving such vanity in his dreary role,
this pervading futility and fatigue he felt,
only the piercing ache of a plaguing hole,
as life's significance only seemed to melt.
He had long defended his kingdom with pride,
but no longer was there any fulfillment to gain,
as senseless existence he began to deride,
while battling despair's unyielding chain.

His life and kingdom now did seem
only inconsequential and fleeting in scope,
as meager as a brief and fading dream,
losing all his old ambitions as he did cope,
and even impending death now did appear
as a sweet liberation from all his anguish,
the final flight from his burden clear,
as he continued now only to languish.

So finally he reached the hermitage far,
after journeying so many days in the cold,
entering the dwelling under many a star,
with growing anticipation now to hold.
Yet the wise hermit could not be found,

with only that vacant home to greet,
with menacing silence, never a sound,
after all that grand eagerness to meet,
and engulfing loneliness he then did bear,
as the knight's vigor quickly did deplete,
that venerable hermit no longer there,
staring with sorrow at his empty seat.

The Appearance

I was pensive on a particular spring day,
contemplating this existence of pain,
walking slowly in my sorrowful way,
with the cruelty of life to only disdain,
when a miraculous Lady did then appear,
my aching soul unready for such a sight,
as her brilliant aura then came near,
left in amazement by her blinding light.
Stunned as her glorious eyes did arrive,
quickly emerging as that destined sign,
her majestic Beauty certainly did derive
from the splendor of the loving Divine,
as I recall again her unique glow,
and her smile which resolved all doubt,
as her unrivaled radiance did flow,
rescuing the land of its drought.

Yet forever from my life she would leave,
never again to see that perfect face,
descending into misery, only to grieve,
bereft of the wonder of her sublime grace.
That separation was too much to bear,
perceiving only a barren and empty cold,
raging again against this existence unfair,
and sinking into that abyss of despair,
yet through all that sorrow which did unfold,
all that mourning which pervaded the air,
her revered Beauty strengthened my trust bold
in the glory of God, in the Infinite which did mold
this cosmos where such a Lady could appear,
where such inspiring marvels I could behold.
Transformed by this experience dear,

as I emerged from that devastating hole,
the universe started to seem more clear,
with new understanding of the lasting soul,
better able to withstand the flooding rain,
crucially rejuvenated, with hope of love,
with stronger endurance of the bitter pain
and a renewed sense of the Infinite above.

The Great Tempest

There is a great tempest in my soul,
this intense chaos without rest,
as the agonizing ache only does grow
with each day of this cruel test,
enduring this harsh existence cold,
with all its inherent sorrow and pain,
while everything we attempt to mold
is only fleeting in this ruthless rain.
And I waver now, as this battle is fought,
between two positions on this turbulent sea.
Firstly there is this utter nihilistic thought,
which strongly compels the need to flee,
perceiving only a meaningless life,
lacking a reason to endure this strife;
and secondly there is my surging hope,
placing my trust in the Infinite higher,
finding my faith in this struggle to cope,
connected to Eternity which does inspire.
And there is vacillation between each side,
in this bewilderment into which I was thrown,
as I endure this misery to which I'm tied,
tortured by this silence, the deep unknown.

Pyrrhus and the Samnite

From the hills of Samnium he came,
the austere Italic sage to finally meet
the renowned general Pyrrhus of fame,
with keen interest as they did greet.

"I'm blessed with the ability innate,
to see moments into the future and past,
and so I understand your current state,
and this present war which you cast.
You who assist the Tarentines in your way
will only find disappointment and dismay,
and yet you resume the ancient feud great
between the Greeks and Trojans old,
as the Romans did descend by fate
from the line of venerable Aeneas bold,
who the rage of Turnus did crucially defeat,
and after many harsh struggles to face,
established in promised Latium his seat,
winning glorious Lavinia to embrace,
her sacred Beauty wondrously profound,
still celebrated, as her radiance did resound,
Beauty naturally a lasting link to the Divine,
enabling our souls with bliss to align.

Yet you who lose too many in battle fierce,
this campaign now you should really forsake,
impossible the city's mighty strength to pierce,
as Rome is destined this world to overtake.
I can see from my high, yet humble home,
the greatness of expanding, valiant Rome,
which will truly dominate for centuries long,
with brilliant minds and courage strong.

You are not fated to succeed in this land,
and should return to Epirus, your plans to mend,
facing now an inevitable superpower grand,
as the pride of Italian might shall always defend.
Resolute Appius Claudius shall never yield,
urging the noble Senate to continue the fight,
always with more inspired troops to wield,
the Republic to rise with its unrivaled height.
But honour my question now, as an elder sage:
why are you always driven such war to wage?"

And so Pyrrhus, holding the man in esteem,
a genuine response thus did provide,
sensing much wisdom, as it did seem,
showing more passion as he did confide.
"I've always been flooded by the desire
to pursue precious glory in my way,
for posterity always to know and admire,
with a grand legacy to conquer death,
with illustrious achievement holding sway,
immortal even after my last breath."

"You seek immortality of that kind,
yet be assured in your stormy mind
that we're all already immortal and Divine,
as known by my predecessors, their line,
the soul always in the serene Realm to last,
while the material body, its sinking mast
quickly falls in that inexorable decay,
while the triumphant core shall always stay.
And what then is glory, but a transient leaf?
Blown by the wind and yet it's the cause

always of such wide turmoil and grief,
as so many neglect to turn and pause
to find that higher connection true,
while enduring and battling through.
So brilliant Pyrrhus, of voracious desire,
you can direct your hunger to a greater end,
commencing with contemplation higher,
and striving your boundless core to mend."

The Lake of Youth

Meditating on my wondrous past,
amidst all these treasured ruins dear,
with such nostalgia for boyhood vast,
swiftly exiled from my home to revere,
I've decided now to attempt a bold return
to the lake of my youth, with waters clear,
longing for peace while I always churn,
recalling wistfully as I venture near,
and I strive valiantly now to revive
the rays of that jubilant, lasting flame,
journeying back where I once did thrive,
towards that bliss to finally reclaim.

The Solitary

The frenzied captain in dismay,
swiftly separated from his great fleet,
was forced now to make his way
towards a nearby island to greet,
his battered ship pushed off course
by tempestuous winds of shattering force.
Skilled at sea, the proud Athenian brave,
against the stubborn Spartans tough,
had long endured the arduous war grave
in this perilous time, through waters rough.
Now distant from the critical action bold,
worried about the flow of the combat grand,
his commitment to Athens he still did hold,
while he was grateful on this island to land.
And with his dutiful men he soon did find
a strange, solitary man who did reside,
bringing much curiosity to the mind,
as the recluse now slowly did confide,
while despondent in his bitter haze,
the crew intrigued by his peculiar past,
observing this man who did cast
his despairing and gloomy gaze.

"You are the first my island to reach
in many long and weary years
and thus I urgently do beseech
amidst all these desolate tears,
that you truly stay and remain
as long as possible, easing my pain.
I was once an adviser to an old king,
a king of Athens in those early days prior,
rejoicing in my role as I did bring

much crucial wisdom and a lofty desire
to best assist my ruler with much insight,
as our city grew, flourishing in might.
I was a seer great, as visions I did behold,
foreseeing both fortune and hardships cold,
but unable to withhold enough of my sight,
too much of the future I did tragically reveal,
uncovering our path, fate's coming flight,
as too much of our destiny I did unseal.
So even as Athens in that day did thrive,
even as my King much prosperity did gain,
enraged Zeus eventually did arrive,
with all his disappointment and disdain.
In his fury, Zeus was quick to proclaim
my horrid punishment as he did exclaim,
and I was exiled to spend my days
in this endless and wretched malaise,
condemned for centuries to this life,
continually battling all this rage ablaze,
alone on this island, with such strife,
utterly destroyed as the barbarians raze,
in this unbearably lonely state,
devastated by all the piercing pain,
and immersed with such mournful hate
for this existence, completely vain.
Abandoned through each aching night,
I question his harshness to deplore,
with this desolation always to fight,
with agony intolerable in my core,
and this crippling loneliness does leave
a cruel hole of such misery intense,
on this barren island only to grieve
with my excruciating pain immense."

Agony

With the constant torment of a vicious fire,
plagued by the Void's agonizing pain,
always dissatisfied as I continue to aspire,
amid the emptiness of the desert to disdain,
existence is always unfulfilled desire,
with so many weary quests only vain,
deteriorating in my anguish as I tire
with my strength difficult to maintain.
I'm ruthlessly bombarded without end,
as each thundering attack does leave
my city devastated, impossible to mend,
trapped in this misery only to grieve,
unable any longer to truly defend
against this vile dread I still perceive,
weakening and powerless to withstand,
constantly battling the relentless strife,
the merciless enemy always in my land,
so enraged by this appalling life.
Still struggling in this cruel unknown,
my wretched condition longing to flee,
I'm losing old hopes, miserably alone,
my ship furiously crippled at sea.
In mournful perplexity and dismay,
it always continues deeply to astound
that God would permit in His way
this excruciating suffering to resound,
while I see only a fleeting ray,
while the pain continues to pound.

Jupiter and Human Pain

Early in Jupiter's proud and majestic reign,
with much sympathy he quickly did realize
that human life involved excessive pain,
hearing the frequent and anguished cries.
So after much contemplative thought,
watching so many their existence deride,
the influence of Venus he then sought,
ordering the goddess then to provide
that jubilantly blissful capacity bold
to experience emotional bonds deep,
the experience of Love, its glory to behold,
to console humans while they weep,
reflective of the joy of the higher sky,
as agreeing Venus was quick to comply,
Jupiter expecting humanity to better endure
their tempestuous lives of weary toil,
more willing to persist on the arduous soil,
before reaching his greater lands pure.

But Minerva, after observing for many years,
long sensitive to the depth of human tears,
reflecting on the human state for much time,
with her profound insight then came
to the opulent palace of Jupiter sublime,
with her renowned wisdom to thus proclaim
that Love, though glorious, was not enough
through desolate human existence rough,
with the underlying pain always to sense,
through all the sorrowful anguish intense.
But though Minerva had showed much force,
by this time Jupiter had ceased to care,
always to perplex on his unknown course,
abandoning humanity in its despair.

The Venetian

"Admiral, we've been on this search too long,
this pursuit which all our energy does drain,
abandoning our trading mission strong,
as now many among the crew disdain
this senseless hunt, this maddening quest,
as you infuriate us with your notions vain,
and our tolerance now you continue to test,
risking a mutiny onboard, a violent stain.
Don't endanger your career, your life so blessed,
as over the years you did ascend and attain
your honourable position and always did aspire
to high achievement, with obligations to maintain.
Think of your duty to Venice, our grand empire,
her growing power, her glorious domain,
your share of that wealth to thus acquire;
think of the Doge, as we rule the seas by fate,
of the Republic serene, our venerable state.
It would be reasonable now to return home,
no longer to chase, to hopelessly roam."

"But what is Venice and duty when all shall perish?
What is the significance of glory and wealth,
when it's all doomed to end, this life I cherish?
Destined for inevitable death, coming with stealth,
I feel that I have awakened in some strange way,
pondering now all that is higher and profound,
and questioning in despair each anguished day,
as Venice's splendor to which I was once bound
no longer keeps me under its former sway,
contemplating now this life, its tragic sound,
furious and distressed in all my dismay.
So we must continue this mission, always bold,
the opportunity much too great to neglect,

with this mighty dream always to hold,
confident that we shall soon detect."

The Admiral had eagerly led the ship on course
for months in search of an ancient shrine renowned,
always proceeding with ardent zeal and force,
never doubting that it would eventually be found.
He heard from a trader in Venice who did contend
that a temple for Juventas, which ancients did raise,
human life in its way did remarkably extend,
on one of the smaller Greek islands to praise.
And so even with the site unknown, difficult to find,
he moved swiftly with great fervor to explore,
and even as his men questioned his mind,
he was always quick their indolence to deplore,
pressing them as another island they did reach,
continuing to probe, rousing the strength of each.

So on this next island, his crew he brought,
walking ahead with his usual hurried pace,
resuming his zealous quest as he sought
this wondrous temple, striving feverishly to trace,
and quickly they encountered a monastery old,
which intrigued enough with its humble grace
to prompt a visit, as their meeting did unfold,
the Admiral permitting a pause in their chase.

"What brings you to our tiny island here,
as you have brought to my peers much fear?
Does Venice desire more land to claim,
advancing again with its military near?
But surely too small for any strategic aim,
we're only quiet monks, a secluded group small,
leading contemplative lives, our desires to tame,
devoted completely to God, the Creator of All."

"We do not come here our power to wield,
but in search of a great remnant of the past,
which promises so jubilantly to yield
a limitless extension of vitality vast;
facing the loss of my youthful Arcadian field,
I yearn as long as possible in this life to last,
against the fragility of existence to shield,
as my cherished hopes so dear I cast
to locate now a revered temple wide,
which immortality will crucially provide."

"Why do you pursue pagan phantoms unwise?
Surely you must with awareness now realize
that your death you cannot evade in disgrace,
an inevitability we all in our time must face."

"I will travel to the ends of the ocean to prevent
my horrid and unjust death, only to lament.
My earthly expiry I will never embrace,
as I will continue always the fight and resist
against vicious Time in this desperate race,
as I long so critically to always persist."

The monk now passionately did reply
with soaring wisdom, inspiring as he did fly.
"But you must overcome this stubborn fear,
as there is no cause to maintain your concern,
as God's glory is within and always near,
soon to joyfully gain that for which you yearn.
So rejoice now, no longer in worry to weep,
knowing that the soul is already immortal in kind,
as you must begin the true search deep
to that endless bliss we're meant to find."

Distant from her Eyes

Now distant from those glorious eyes,
her radiance never again to behold,
I'm trapped in this agony to despise,
in this always empty and grueling cold,
recalling that smile which did amaze,
which lifted my soaring soul for days,
now in tormenting solitude as I mourn,
battered by anguish and always forlorn.
Though I knew her only for a time brief,
in torturous tempests I'm caught,
through this vast and unrelenting grief,
always flooded and utterly distraught.
Ravaged is my beleaguered boat
in these vicious waters immense,
with those eyes so painfully remote,
always battered with this ache intense,
with this hopeless lack, always bereft,
through this arduous trial of length,
in this desolate darkness left,
struggling with diminishing strength.
And no longer can I truly sustain
the perilous waves of this cruel sea,
reaching my threshold as I wane,
as I long now to finally flee.

The Hermit

"Lacking any perceptible purpose clear,
this weary life I don't comprehend,
always enduring this misery as I steer
through this vile emptiness to contend.
We face mighty floods which ravage
and plagues which arrive in stealth,
ruthless invaders, swiftly savage,
diminishing our fleeting health;
we meet each earthquake and storm,
destroying our dear structures grand,
so quickly losing that youthful form,
left in the despair of this dire land,
while death is always so near,
rendering our efforts merely vain,
filling so many with aching fear,
and that anguish, always to chain.
As only futile seems each path,
I must question this maddening life,
the nothingness only bringing wrath,
always trapped in this useless strife."

Hearing his sorrowful visitor's cry,
now the hermit did caringly reply.
"Though life brings inevitable grief,
you must venture deeper in your way:
think not of the single struggling leaf,
thrown by the wind in its lonely dismay,
but of the entire forest, majestic and vast,
which through the years shall always last.
With silence you must strive to converse,
beyond the tempest, the surface storm,
and into the sea's depths you can traverse

finding your true core of immortal form,
your radiant identity always serene,
full of endless joy and inspired might,
as childhood fields wondrously green,
always linked to the Divine's height.
And when your sorrow happens to swell,
you can return to this blessed well,
this cherished sanctuary fortified,
which to the Source is always tied.
Our loving home is beyond the skies,
and it is critical now for you to start
to directly and jubilantly realize
that you are a crucially sacred part
of the glorious Infinite which does reign,
that Eternal consciousness High,
meant to ascend through each plane
towards the supreme bliss as you fly."

Empedocles

Empedocles to one of his pupils great
with urgency began a crucial discourse,
closer now to his final day of fate,
conversing with much passionate force.
"I truly believe that it's now time,
as you are ready for greater light,
as I shall reveal mysteries sublime,
into the Divine with more insight.
I have travelled to many a distant land,
to great Egypt and into the East,
meeting those who seem to feast
on knowledge of the gods grand.
And many of the sick I have healed
all over our island with focus brave,
as many in crippling illness reeled
until I ended a plague once-grave.

But weary now of life with all its pain,
I feel my mission complete as a sage,
as I long to return to the joyful Domain,
ready to flee this miserable stage.
But before I end this particular life,
facing my agonizing inner storm
and enduring much deep strife,
it is critical now that I do inform,
with more of my wisdom to reveal,
vital for your soul, on its journey to heal.

Know that we were once blissful spirits high,
as in that wondrous Realm we did dwell,
until a mournful transgression, an error to decry,
when we then quickly and tragically fell
into this desolate land, losing the sublime,

punished with a series of incarnations here,
incurring this struggle for that enigmatic crime,
into this world where agony is always near,
to this corrupt plain as we did descend,
as we work for our suffering souls to mend.
So we're wandering selfishly now in exile,
clothed in these painful bodies to despise,
facing multiple lives, each an arduous trial,
striving to develop into higher sages wise,
but after many lives in which to learn,
we can then break free of this cyclic test
by finally making that crucial inward turn
and recognizing our innate glory to soar,
finally able in Eternity to joyfully rest,
and united with that bliss forevermore.
So as the other bold sages do affirm,
the immortality of the soul I must confirm,
as eventually to that Realm we shall return,
as we all truly and inherently yearn.
Thus you must ignore the material and vain,
and attend to your core, as it does grow,
with your focus on the Eternal to maintain,
devoted to the purifying waters which flow."

Responding in his way quite keen,
the pupil was now ready to intervene.
"But causing many tears as I grieve,
why this life must you now suddenly leave?
I shall always deeply venerate and adore,
but why not share your wisdom with more?
And distressed by such a plan to sustain,
why must we face so many lives of pain?
It's excessive suffering on this wretched soil,
with so much misery and exhausting toil."

"I too sense the harshness of the design,
as less pain we all so ardently desire,
but it was decreed in the eons prior,
by all the gods in their plan Divine.
Yet the pain leads to cleansing of the soul,
as this grueling voyage we must embrace,
as suffering often compels us with its toll
towards the pursuit of sweet liberation pure,
to be free of the long bondage we face,
as the yearning for knowledge begins to stir.

Yet understand now that I've sunk into despair,
and my wisdom I already did work to share
with the few open and willing to receive,
as the hedonistic masses are mostly blind,
as their intrinsic divinity they don't perceive,
unwilling their core to contemplate nor find,
trapped always insatiably in the mundane,
too busy with the insignificant and vain,
or working in hubris for humanity to advance,
unaware of the inadequacy of their trance.
Now tired of this land as I languish,
I feel I've completed this round's quest,
in this aching body with all its anguish,
so hungry for that most serene rest.
So it is time for my death at Etna high,
with that harmonious joy my desire,
for my immortal soul now to fly,
preparing to enter that volcanic fire.
We shall unite again in the days ahead,
in the jubilant Realm, soaring above,
as death itself you must never dread,
protected always by that highest Love."

Stunned

I was walking in my gloomy way,
with such despair and dwindling hope,
through another tormenting day,
always with that harsh agony to cope,
when in a moment to always prize,
illuminated by these sudden rays,
I swiftly saw those great brown eyes,
so stunned in my wondrous daze.
Even in my sorrow then so great,
her inspiring Beauty did remind,
through my besieged and weary state,
even as I battled my tortured mind,
that there was truly a meaning deep
through all our afflictions as we weep,
and struggling with my excruciating ache,
fighting through the mundane sleep,
I was lifted by her eyes as I did awake
to the Transcendent which does surround,
God's majesty which never does forsake,
His boundless Love always to abound.
And though the experience did not last,
fleetingly aware of the Ultimate Ground,
I was connected to that blissful peace vast,
while triumphant jubilation did resound,
contemplating the Realm which did mold
the ideal glory of her perfect face,
as I was blessed that day to behold
that inspiring gift of sacred grace.

Warrior of the North

There was a valiant warrior of the North,
by his tribe honoured and deeply adored,
who into many fierce battles went forth
and against his enemies always soared.
But after several victories, many a conquest,
he became arrogant, growing in pride,
as the tolerance of the gods he would test,
all his imprudent behavior to deride;
as his territory he greedily did expand,
as a god himself he then did conceive,
and worship from his men he did demand,
only lusting for more power to perceive.
And soon high Odin he quickly did offend,
who then his favour furiously withdrew,
as a reprimand the god would send,
as his rage then increasingly grew.

So to Midgard Odin decided to travel down,
with his stern punishment to exclaim,
visiting the proud warrior in his town,
as he was still basking in his tribal fame.
"For your disappointing conduct of disgrace,
the cold, treacherous waters you will cross,
as I've decided now an exile you will face,
as long storms your vessel will toss,
your audacity producing such disdain,
as only in lonely sorrow you will roam,
to live now with a remote people in pain,
always far from your cherished home."

The Freedom of Youth

Before the abyss, my anguish of fate,
before my existence I did deplore,
I truly rejoiced in a blissful state,
in my joyous childhood, free to soar.
With that liberty, such a wondrous time,
there was always that elation to greet
in that cherished era, so sublime,
with all those fruits always sweet.

Running through the vibrant green,
I was blessed without any stain,
immersed in that peace serene,
free from all this sorrow and pain.
Content merely with friends to play,
I roamed through many a sacred field,
amidst Nature's generous sway,
exploring with such energy to wield,
the shepherds smiling in their way,
the harvest always abundant in its yield,
as the Sun's nurturing rays did beam,
in immense delight as I did gleam.

And I was free of Love's agony deep,
which leaves me now in desolation to burn,
that tormenting ache as I often weep,
while my veneration they don't return.
With my sensitivity to Beauty profound,
immobilized for long days as I do reel,
I'm dazed so often as it does astound,
with all these wounds which never heal.
Now enduring this continued descent,
impossible to that pure glory to return,
I'm trapped in this cave where I was sent,
as all this anguish continues to churn.

Polyphemus

Solitary in his dreary cave,
miserable Polyphemus did dwell,
always battling his condition grave,
as his deep anguish did swell,
now compelled again to lament,
as he was heard far into the sea,
weary of his ceaseless torment,
his existence longing to flee.

"Her beauty so long I did adore,
that wondrous nymph so fair,
but now Love itself I must deplore,
abandoned in devastating despair.
To win cherished Galatea I did fail,
as this lonely isolation does inflame,
in this wretched agony as I wail,
my wrath now unable to tame,
as this surging fury does burn,
tired of life's absurd game,
recalling her cruelty as she did spurn
my advances when I did proclaim
my venerating devotion complete,
with sacred unity as my aim.
When her majestic glory I did greet,
I was always in that astonished haze,
honoured then merely to stand
near her stunning celestial rays,
with those illuminating eyes grand,
in her Divine presence high,
captivated by her graceful ways,
and clearly blessed by the sky.

Left with this piercing ache intense,
I've flooded this land with my tears,
in this torturing void immense,
enduring this sorrow for years.
That visitor Telemus, truly wise,
remarkably gifted with such sight,
in early days so quickly did recognize
my inevitable grief and plaguing plight,
the depth of this lovesick stain,
and this loneliness to so disdain.
So in this bleak darkness further I sink,
immersed in this unbearable scourge,
descending to some dreadful brink,
with a fierce eruption on the verge,
as the volcano ominously near,
as even the gods soon shall fear.

Flawed Zeus I must resent,
who enslaves us here to decay,
while our hardships never relent,
while we struggle each grueling day,
as I must scorn his ruthless reign,
sickened by merciless Love cruel,
trapped in this suffering and pain,
while that indifferent tyrant does rule.
He allows such constant strife
to overwhelm so many a humble life,
provoking my powerful rage,
to unleash my rampaging force,
to break life's imprisoning cage,
and attack on a vicious course.

Now undaunted in my furious might,
I must gather all the willing and proud,
all the Cyclopes, readying to fight
with all our valiant armies loud,
against the corrupt Olympians to rebel,
their mountain to boldly scale,
in our noble revolt to work to expel
unjust Zeus, destructive in our trail,
as the desperate battles shall flow,
that regent merely a deity low,
an errant being, ruthlessly cold,
who jealously strives his seat to hold,
punishing us in this wilderness dire,
only subordinate to gods even higher.
So we must summon now the strength
all those old fortifications to breach,
to endure a crucial war of length,
his palace to finally reach."

Numa's Visitor

On campaign, two Romans encamped at night,
always waiting for the next battle to arise,
were conversing now on their common plight,
their perilous lives no longer to prize,
constantly preparing for an enemy force,
and acutely aware of fate's fragile course.

"This existence my friend now does tire,
always on this cruel march, increasingly dire.
As I've ventured to many a remote plain,
to high duty I've always been allied,
for the Republic's glory, enduring much pain,
fighting for Rome with honour and pride,
yet always facing another ominous fight,
now from life itself I begin to recoil,
lacking the vigor of youth, a fading light,
in this endless struggle, this weary toil."

Relating to his companion's cry,
the second Roman did promptly reply.
"I heard of a certain Greek who I can report,
who once audaciously visited Numa's court.
Recall now wise Numa, our second King,
before our great Republic did spring,
succeeding Romulus, taking the throne,
who in matters sacred was renowned,
with his revered wisdom and pious tone,
with many rites and institutions to found,
who as a guardian of peace was always keen,
and often from Egeria much insight did glean.
So Numa was shocked by this Greek bold,

an ardent traveller with much knowledge old,
a mysterious figure who in his many years
claimed to have met with numerous seers.
So Numa warmly welcomed his guest,
ready to discuss and the Greek's aptitudes test,
yet he had come for assistance in his expedition,
quickly explaining the urgency of his mission.
On his way north to the Alps, he was in search
of another sage on a towering mountain's perch,
and with fervent enthusiasm he did maintain
that secrets of the cosmos this sage did ascertain.
Now this recluse he was determined to find,
such passion always fuelling his curious fire,
as such mysteries had long plagued his mind,
as on many matters he was ready to inquire.
Willing to share the knowledge upon his return,
for a group of escorting soldiers he did yearn,
to provide protection on his northward quest,
as Numa considered the intriguing request.

So the King went to Egeria for guidance to gain,
long trusting her noble counsel to hear,
but Egeria was quick to denounce and restrain,
filled suddenly with much overwhelming fear.
Roman men she advised strongly not to send,
as it was forbidden by Jupiter that mount to ascend.
Thus worried Numa, always pious in his way,
swiftly refused the offer, to the Greek's dismay,
warning the traveller not that sage to approach,
to avoid the fury of the gods, their reproach.
Yet the Greek was unmoved, ready to march,

even as Numa attempted to dissuade,
disappointed as he left the Roman arch,
still as zealous as a fierce barbarian raid.

So eventually to the foot of the Alps he did arrive,
ready with his boundless questions deep,
yet soon he would struggle just to survive,
crushed with anguish as he did weep.
Quickly a furious giant on his path did emerge,
as such erupting panic then did flow,
a relative of Cacus bringing him to the verge
of a cruel death in the isolated snow.
Yet he managed frantically to flee,
running into the distance with all his speed,
finding a forest, many a covering tree,
from this giant's rage finally freed.

After several days, he believed he was then near
to the sage, knowledge of the higher sphere,
yet as he climbed with zeal to the cherished height,
he was soon thwarted by Jupiter's furious might,
the Greek then distraught with his flood of tears,
as Jupiter his punishment did sternly announce,
to endure slave labour for the rest of his years,
as his actions the god did swiftly denounce,
with such unceasing sorrow then to bear,
forced to face that relentless despair.
Thus to a remote king he was then bound,
painfully distant from his adored home,
condemned in this way which did confound,
never again his native plains to roam."

Profound Yearning

I sense this profoundly vast desire,
which can never be satisfied here,
as we're meant for that Realm Higher,
Eternity to triumph over death and fear;
through many years we strive to mend,
towards that cherished summit to return,
destined for that joy which does transcend,
as for the Absolute we innately yearn.
Restless and weary of this remote plain,
with this desolate wilderness to endure,
yet my courage I aspire to maintain,
as I long for my true home pure,
and my deep emptiness does reveal,
as I now quest for that purity of sight,
that this void only the Infinite can heal,
when with that bliss I finally unite.

Her Glorious Eyes

Wandering, I was despondent and alone
when she so wondrously did appear,
taking me to that precious peak unknown,
as for that brief moment all seemed clear.
Disillusioned, my battered ship was adrift,
when my resurgent hopes so swiftly grew,
as to a new state she promptly did lift,
and my mind as a majestic eagle flew,
finding so suddenly those striking eyes,
and her Divine smile as I did gaze,
in elation as I was soaring in the skies,
momentarily free from life's cruel maze,
in complete awe as I reeled in her sight,
with such illumination difficult to bear,
unprepared for that radiant height,
the beginnings of Love already there.

But despite my all my veneration deep,
she is always beyond my struggling reach,
left in this agonizing sorrow to weep,
as my city's walls have suffered a breach,
no longer able to defend each raid,
and burdened by this distressing fight,
as my diminishing energies only fade,
always destined for more plight.
And though I'm struggling with much pain,
she awakened my soul, with ardent might,
reassured by my knowledge to maintain,
after that transcending day of sacred flight.
Through sorrow, I'm strengthened to know,
in this quiet contemplation, inspired to rise,
that cherished Beauty shall always flow,
with solace in her glorious eyes.

Wrath

A Roman, who honour had always sought,
fighting Rome's enemies on many a plain,
was struck by a dreaded plague, left distraught
with this horrific illness to then sustain.
Questioning the gods, his misery did abound,
as he lamented his condition in furious pain,
a satisfying life no longer to be found,
his political aspirations unable to attain.

To venture to Cumae he then did decide,
managing slowly to travel arduously down,
always with the oppressive illness to deride,
as he eventually reached the sacred town.
He was eager to see the renowned Sibyl old,
keen for some divine insight to hear,
explaining the entirety of his affliction cold,
approaching the venerable priestess dear.

"I come to you in my bleak dismay,
attacked by this cruel illness I despise,
incomprehensible to suffer in such a way,
mourning old dreams and each lost prize.
My life in ruins, I'm utterly perplexed
that I must face this tormenting fate,
this mournful disease leaving me vexed,
bewildered by my deteriorating state.
In my distress, with so many tears,
I'm left merely to struggle and weep,
but I turn to your wisdom of many years
to probe into this mystery so deep."

Sympathetic to his painful cry,
thus the Sibyl did solemnly reply.
"As I delve into your suffering's source,
I see that one of your ancestors went astray,
provoking punitive action of much force,
your lineage revealing a disobedient way.
Your family from Sybaris does descend,
where once a ruler incurred Apollo's wrath,
his relations with the Divine not willing to mend,
bequeathing to his sons a torturous path.
Sybaris for its wide corruption was known,
with its hedonistic ways, its luxury vain,
such desertion of duty to bemoan,
that impiety and decadence to disdain.

To build a great temple Apollo did request,
promising to protect the colony as it did expand,
but the city's ruler the gods' power did detest,
taking an audacious and defiant stand.
The gods he never did trust nor fear,
using his resources instead to boldly train
a substantial army which he would revere,
with more influential strength to gain,
augmenting his palace which did tower,
enjoying his wealth and prosperous reign,
focusing only on the extension of his power,
and bounded only to the material to attain.
Apollo was deeply angered by this neglect,
quickly punishing the ruler with an illness grave,
as such rebellious disgrace he rarely did detect,
the plague then spreading with its deadly wave.
And even some descendants of this Sybarite unwise
were then struck with this plague, a cruel demise."

"To be punished for my ancestor's offence
is an absurd injustice which I can't comprehend,
only producing more erupting fury intense,
as only more agony the gods seem to send.
This world is too flawed, its horrid design clear,
as this existence always illness does stain,
with undue suffering, each mournful tear,
the gods not worthy of worship in this pain.
And with this ancestral transgression's cost,
with all this sorrow I'm forced to endure,
the meaning of higher duty now seems lost,
always in anguish as I continue to stir."

Cherished Meeting

Recalling our cherished meeting dear,
the way her cosmic splendor did teem,
her unequalled radiance I'll always revere,
her celestial wonder as she did beam;
unable to stay in her overpowering light,
after witnessing that emanating glow,
that shocked haze continued to flow
even several days after her sight,
as she provided fleeting insight clear,
and melted all the impeding snow,
beyond the illusory veil to finally peer,
towards that understanding to grow.
And her perfection which did shine
fortified my hope as I bravely did steer,
revealing the glory of the sacred design,
and quickly vanquishing all my fear.

In Misery

I mourn this miserable life of tears,
this existence only natural to resent,
through all these anguished years,
united with all those who lament;
so in this excruciating human state,
once fleeting youth is swiftly spent,
we're condemned to this harsh fate,
this empty and disappointing descent,
with the distress of unfulfilled desire,
and all the underlying sorrow innate,
with dissatisfaction's raging fire,
still trapped in this wretched state.

Consciousness brings constant pain,
our species insignificant as we despair,
while the tedious labour seems only vain,
with all this restless boredom to bear,
with the useless absurdity of it all,
as the dying birds only transiently fly,
old hopes crumbling as castles fall,
with dreaded blizzards from the sky.
Always obscured is the summit far,
so remote while I endure this lack,
as I've been left with too many a scar,
the snow's barrage continuing to attack,
and as the grief continues to teem,
its vast excessiveness to so disdain,
the boundless suffering now does seem
to render this life too painful to remain.
So left without any clarity dear,
amid this frozen desolation forlorn,
with the ruthless winds always near,
I continue in my misery to mourn.

The Lament of Titus

I'm compelled now ceaselessly to weep,
sinking without any hope to glean,
my beloved Berenice unable to keep,
many too suspicious of a foreign queen.
Her eyes wondrously Divine as I recall,
and her glory unmatched in the empire,
yet into these excruciating depths I fall,
battling this deep and unceasing fire,
this endless war unbearable to sustain,
the burden of such unfulfilled desire,
as all my high duties seem only vain,
deteriorating each hour as I tire.
Ailing in this venerable palace seat,
it's useless this highest power to hold
when each day this misery I must meet,
so crippled by this brutal cold.

The gods are capricious in their way,
perhaps even indifferent to our cries,
in this existence of such dismay,
so easy in this resentment to despise.
Rome's greatness, which I long did revere,
which inspired such ardent ambition high,
has lost its cherished appeal, once so dear,
as I often stare now at the inscrutable sky.
Her memory only more pain does bring,
condemned in this torment to languish,
thus only in lamentation do I sing,
drowning further in this lonely anguish,
and now losing my will and desire,
I seem to be dying of this despair,
alone in this wretched desert dire,
no longer able this life to bear.

Among all these Ruins

Among all these ruins I now lament,
as this deep sorrow does pervade,
still contemplating my swift descent,
the day that cruel anguish did invade.
Vanishing quickly were those jubilant days,
as that blissful era I mournfully recall,
banished from all those triumphant ways,
the empire of youth destined to fall.
With the collapse of boyhood's years,
my capital swiftly ravaged to the ground,
existence is now only agony and tears,
lacking the trumpet's gallant sound,
as the barbarians stormed into our land,
the grieving eagle in its last hours of flight,
the fortifications no longer to stand,
as I wept through that shocking night.
And as all this devastation does surround,
never again to reach that majestic height,
only plaguing torment does abound,
always to grieve for my former might.

The Return

There was a son of a King great,
raised in a vast kingdom of peace,
where he enjoyed his jubilant state,
where the bliss never did cease,
as he was cherished in this land,
his glorious home to adore,
as his joy always did expand,
able in euphoria to freely soar.

Yet soon the son ardently did desire
his own proud kingdom to create,
with aspirations as he did aspire
from his old father to separate,
deeply yearning for his own strength,
for satisfying power to craft and hold,
to build a grand empire of length,
to experience independence bold.
The King promptly then did decide
to exile his son to an island small,
no longer a connection to provide,
the conditions quickly to appall.

Now facing many a grueling trial,
far from his father's embrace,
the son struggled on this isle,
with perilous suffering to face.
And yet slowly in the unknown,
the son did gradually work to raise
a growing kingdom of his own,
tenacious through those long days,
building many structures high,
flourishing during his reign,
with new opportunities to fly,
advancing as he did maintain

his goals of unceasing ambition,
all his desires longing to gain,
progressing with each lofty mission,
always labouring through the pain.

However the son soon did realize
that his realm could never equate,
aching now under the difficult skies,
as he started sinking with his weight.
Unable lasting fulfillment to find,
always empty as he did seek,
he searched his restless mind,
growing now more pensively meek.

Finally the son decided to leave
his kingdom and everything he knew,
weary of existence as he did grieve,
as a deeper mission now swiftly grew.
So he set out to the sea cold,
striving now to make his return,
for his father's kingdom to behold,
for all that old bliss as he did yearn.
Through the wind as it did roar,
through all the tempests of fear,
he found hope in his inspired core,
with greater fortitude to steer.
More warmth the Sun did provide
as his ship crossed each wave,
and the brilliant stars did guide
his devoted path, always brave.
So from all his suffering to flee,
long traversing with resilient might,
he continued his voyage at sea,
on that quest for his father's height.

With Marcus Aurelius

You must find fortitude, fellow Roman brave,
as you continue on your honourable way,
securing liberation from this misery grave,
gathering stronger legions amid your dismay.
Even as you face each ruthless raid,
attacked relentlessly each dreary day,
your strength on campaign must never fade,
with tenacious defenses always to stay;
you must not allow the emotions which invade,
even with this desolate agony you face,
to really disturb your deeper tranquil state,
that peaceful fortress within to embrace,
as you work to recognize Divine Fate,
the workings of Providence to trace.
With the harmonious cosmos aligned,
you shall cultivate more courage bold,
striving valiantly to fortify your mind,
continuing to cherish the sages of old,
with thoughts more resilient and pure,
as you aspire all your sorrow to endure.
Though now life itself you long to flee,
your mind you can truly labour to train,
endeavouring to be wondrously free
from any affliction on this fleeting plain,
and surely you shall be triumphant in time,
as you realize your deeper and cosmic sight,
recognizing in vast nature the sublime,
and transcending your pain with new might.

Perplexed

Perplexed by this universe cruel,
the Divine plan bewildering in its way,
the unknown only continues to fuel
more restless anguish each day.
Did I agree to this life, to be born,
knowing all the misery I would endure,
knowing that I would always mourn,
as I descended from those fields pure?
Before this life, did I have a choice,
a free and honoured individual voice?
Or was I condemned to suffer in this land,
falling into sorrow, forced to withstand?
But why was it not possible to remain
in that always serene and joyful place,
in the glory of that wondrous Domain,
without this plaguing grief to face?
I still push all these boulders of weight,
always struggling on this miserable plain;
yet why was it necessary to create
this vast cosmos of boundless pain?

The Warning of Tiresias

I'm deeply troubled with what I see,
as the future generations will clearly flee
from the Metaphysical and the Divine,
no longer with the Infinite to align.
To my utter perplexity and dismay,
it appears that they will lose their sight,
blinded by absorbed hubris as they decay,
unable to perceive the summit's height,
as into nothingness they will descend,
with empty desires and a void so vast,
in those precarious winds, difficult to mend,
with that despair and anguish to cast,
neglecting the glory of the higher Domain,
lacking trust in ultimate meaning to soar,
in the cherished Love which does sustain,
and forgetting the foundation in their core.
The masses shall turn to the material and vain,
trapped in a petty cycle of voracious greed,
but it's deep knowledge that they must regain,
recognizing the eternal soul's greatest need;
thus back to the Divine they must turn,
back to all the venerable sages great,
who knew our true and everlasting state,
that bliss for which we all do yearn.
They must trust the sacred wisdom old,
as only dissatisfaction will flow in the mind,
critical to recover from that desolate cold,
their immortal radiance again to find.

A Tuscan's Vision

Two medieval Tuscans now did walk
to young Florence on their way,
engaged deeply in their long talk,
approaching on this illuminated day.

"I had a recent vision of Florence great,
which is destined so wondrously to grow
with stunning splendor which does await,
as the brilliance of Italian genius shall flow.
Still developing now is the budding town,
but in the arts it shall flourish and teem,
to be known through Europe with renown,
with such cultural greatness supreme;
with other Italian cities to compete,
it will be the pride of Italy to resound,
with such illustrious glory to greet,
ascending with aspirations profound,
and soon with its confidence to flower,
with new regard for the human to sound,
it will gain in prosperity and power,
the jubilant rebirth to truly astound.
The spirited city-state will always strive
with its reverence for the ancients bold,
expanding valiantly as it will soon thrive,
valuing individual achievements to mold,
as an honored leader will then arrive,
with his grand ambitions to hold,
bringing even more radiant light,
a great patron of the arts high,
blessed with his impressive sight,
enabling the Florentines to truly fly.
As the Magnificent he will be known,

of a prestigious house to prevail,
his deeper appreciation to be shown,
on his lofty course as he must sail.

So Florence shall soon produce in time,
with its intellectual pursuits to revere,
remarkable art and literature sublime,
lasting achievements always dear,
the majestic trumpets then to hear,
attracting many a scholar and sage,
as the artists and writers will steer
swiftly into this blooming golden age.
Many will be rejuvenated as they aspire,
in this cherished city to always adore,
miraculous minds reaching planes higher,
as triumphant birds determined to soar,
the beloved city continually to inspire
with that Beauty connected to our core.
Showing the power of the sacred mind,
the creation of Beauty reveals the Divine,
art as a truly meaningful vocation to find,
as its contemplation then helps us to align
with the Eternal, with the Infinite Love,
with the transcendence of God Above;
these immortal achievements will endure,
these cultural wonders to deeply prize,
remembered even in the Kingdom pure,
as all of wondrous Italy soon shall rise."

The Centurion

"Centurion, how do you remain so brave,
vanquishing so easily all your fear,
through this dreadful war so grave,
with pain and death so near?"

"We have a duty our pain to bear
on this devoted climb, never to bend,
striving to reach that joyous air,
purifying the soul as it must mend.
And our cherished civilization, our home
we must always labour to defend,
against the vile barbarians to contend,
protecting the glory of triumphant Rome.
Through many arduous campaigns cold,
death's inevitable hour I no longer fear,
as I will always remember and hold
that revered wisdom which I did hear,
the perpetual wisdom which does assure
of our eternal essence to always endure.

When the tough Samnites we did fight
in the venerable Republic's early days,
those resilient warriors showing much might,
requiring a large army to subdue and raze,
to consult the Oracle our ancestors did decide,
the Pythia venerated with much esteem,
and the Delphic priestess thus did provide
certain directions to our eager regime,
to raise statues honouring Greeks of old,
the bravest and wisest of the mold.
And so the Romans of the day did proceed,
choosing Alcibiades and Pythagoras great,

building in the forum with swift speed,
further glorifying our city and state,
with brilliant Pythagoras long to admire,
his excellence as vast as the endless sea,
his wondrous teachings always to inspire,
providing that crucial road to be free.

So you must recall the noble thought
of radiant Pythagoras who always sought
the knowledge of transcendent height,
illuminating the land with his vast light,
and thus your fears you can then tame,
as our immortality he did securely proclaim,
the voyaging soul imperishable in kind,
with hope in Eternity to ease the mind.
The valiant soul must bear its journey long,
the toil of this aching existence not in vain,
through these difficult lives growing strong,
preparing to join the celestial plane.
Pythagoras then inspired Plato Divine,
uncovering that lasting temple deep,
as all the great sages in their wisdom align,
towards that beaming knowledge to reap.
Thus you can calm your storms which flow,
with trust in the ancient teachings grand,
as you are meant your core to know,
soon to reside in that blissful land."

In Battle

There's always deep pain to bear,
constantly fighting the merciless strife,
flooded by this intensifying despair,
entirely disillusioned with this life,
so enraged by all this torment,
and forsaken now as I only mourn,
while the enemy armies never relent
in this existence which I scorn.
As these invasions never cease,
there's always another battle ahead,
still yearning for that elusive peace,
while I refortify in constant dread,
as I'm trapped on this darkening field,
lacking the energies now to defend,
with the piercing sorrow never to yield,
as further into the void I descend.

Towards Meaning

When my precious mission I pursue,
my soul's cherished task on this plain,
towards more meaning to finally align,
the joy is then victorious over the pain,
as I notice each synchronous sign,
with rejuvenating energies to accrue,
with greater connection to the Divine,
as I'm better able then to sustain
the intrinsic suffering of this land,
striving towards that boundless shine,
as I aspire the emptiness to subdue,
towards that mountain always clear,
with renewed fortifications to stand
and that blissful fountain dear.

The Hermit's Address

Have courage through your suffering state,
through your many battles and the fire,
as this existence you must not berate,
trusting truly that there's purpose higher
underlying the cosmos even as you grieve,
with the crucial duty to strive to endure
through life's full term as you now achieve,
always united with those lands pure.
Aspire now to be resilient and brave,
with that deeper tranquility to locate,
even in this arduous condition grave,
as your were born to soar and create,
as your core with the cosmos must align,
through your struggle with hope to maintain,
finding that which provides meaning Divine,
your joyful mission of which you're aware,
your task which the Infinite did ordain,
which shall rejuvenate, as you must bear,
which shall inspire your sight past the veil,
with much to accomplish as I beseech,
meant with your fortified strength to sail,
recognizing the transience of each bane,
voyaging towards that shore to reach,
to your lasting citadel beyond the pain.

Excruciating

As forced labour under a tyrant's rule,
never able this desolation to flee,
this excruciating existence is only cruel,
always battered by this punishing sea.
With meager drops of joy, never to last,
everything is meaningless on this campaign,
in this tempestuous ocean, agonizingly vast,
in this restless ennui which does chain,
with serenity so fleeting, lacking that peace,
in perpetual war, toiling miserably in vain,
amidst my piercing sorrow, never to cease,
imprisoned here on this lower plane.
Tragically crippled was my mighty fleet,
as the merciless winds continue to invade,
with only this vile loneliness to meet,
plagued by this emptiness as I fade,
and with true fulfillment impossible to find,
with this voyage too difficult to bear,
I'm always afflicted by my weary mind,
sinking in this boundless despair.

Her Brilliant Eyes

I was stunned when I saw her face,
utterly dazed as she did astound,
as she walked with inspiring grace
with those beams of wonder profound.
Temporarily free of the desolate cold,
her eyes were so luminous in their way,
reminding then of radiant Diotima of old,
rescued on that weary and tedious day,
and as I witnessed her renewing smile,
far from this empty desert I did soar,
away from this mundane land vile,
with ardent wings in my deepest core.
Unable amidst such glory to cope,
soon I was returning back down,
into the usual abyss which does drown,
yet revitalized with vigorous hope.
Quickly vanishing, she shockingly left,
never again her eminence to find,
leaving me in bitter anguish bereft,
and plagued by my mournful mind,
yet though I'm still painfully adrift,
her brilliant eyes I shall always recall,
the way my inspired soul she did lift,
aligned briefly with the Source of all.

The Wanderer

Arriving strangely at the port,
the ancient sailor with intense eyes
commenced frantically to exhort,
rapidly gathering a group to rise.
"I come to relate my profound past,
the depths of my sorrow to share,
the cruelty which Jupiter did cast,
and the source of all my despair.
I have this memory which does remain
of my peaceful consciousness prior
to this human existence which I disdain,
before the agony of this raging fire.
Though I was forced from Lethe to drink,
into this corrupt world then to sink,
I'm still able some moments to recall
before my descent, that regrettable fall.

I was in the joyful kingdom higher,
amidst these marvels to so treasure,
free of all grief and unfulfilled desire,
basking in this vastness beyond measure.
But in curiosity, I noticed the world below,
sympathetic to humanity's suffering deep,
noticing the flooding pain which did flow
and all the agony as so many did weep.
So I decided then to question Jupiter high,
asserting that the cosmos was unsound,
my numerous questions continuing to fly,
as my protest against suffering did resound.
But Jupiter would no longer tolerate my cries
and quickly a punishment he did proclaim,
sending me down from those serene skies,

with much disappointment as he did exclaim.
Thus I was condemned to this human life,
but one especially filled with anguish,
forced to battle such relentless strife,
to always wander this sea as I languish,
and so I traverse these waters alone,
with this loneliness which does torment,
shocked by the harshness which was shown,
enduring this sentence to deeply resent.
The pain leaves me in a bleak state,
devoid of much energy and strength,
truly perplexed by my woeful fate,
through these dreary years of length,
and so I visit various cities around the sea,
seeking relief from the storms to fear,
attempting my vile loneliness to flee,
and sharing my sorrow for more to hear."

A Glimpse

I was immersed in nothingness complete,
sensing only tedious futility on this plain,
with only that meaninglessness to meet,
scorning all as merely useless and vain,
when after my long solitude intense,
after vast suffering as I did weep,
contemplating in that silence immense,
I then had a glimpse of knowledge deep,
that soaring bliss, gloriously profound,
beyond the mundane to transcend,
briefly uniting as all did resound,
and newly aware, as I did ascend.

Childhood Joy

Recalling my cherished childhood of joy,
with triumphant euphoria in the air,
chasing each victory as a jubilant boy,
with never any tedium nor despair,
I soared as a blissful eagle in flight,
completely immersed in ecstatic play,
with that flourishing energy of might,
those boundless dreams each day.

The Longing Within

I sense in my depths profound
such a wondrously higher need,
as my mounting Love does resound,
on which all my hopes do feed,
this desire sacred and innate,
as my core now strives to align,
this longing within so great,
my yearning for the Infinite Divine,
as all my anguish will only cease
when finally with Eternity I unite,
in that joyful, jubilant peace,
meant to aspire to that sight.

In the Cold

Walking in this harsh cold,
far from the Sun's treasured rays,
my hopes I'm unable to hold,
losing that might of prior days.
Not even the trees here rise,
in the wretchedness of this place,
as I recall the radiance of her eyes,
and the glory of her stunning face.
Trapped in this punishing clime,
isolated from her higher grace,
I miss her intellect sublime,
that former joy we did embrace.
Unable this cosmos to understand,
I'm tired of this life's bleak trial,
as I despise this frozen land,
this barren tundra only vile,
useless as this existence vain,
as I continue in anguish to sink,
impossible to bear all this pain,
and not destined to joyously drink
from Love's elusive fountain high,
as I reach agony's perilous brink,
declining in this desolate way,
as the dear birds no longer fly,
in this cruel cold as I decay,
as I lament to the silent sky.

Striving at Sea

Amid this harsh sea agonizingly vast,
this boundless emptiness to disdain,
recalling disappointments of the past,
I long to transcend now all this pain,
to aspire towards that crucial sight,
past this stubborn fog to finally know,
journeying each day with renewed might
to the dear city which always does glow.
My small vessel struck by each wave,
through all the daunting gales which stir,
I strive for that port which will save,
to finally unite with the harbor pure.

Tiberinus

When old Tiberinus Silvius did reign,
venerable Alba Longa's mighty King,
many joyful festivities he would ordain,
often celebrating his love, blissfully to sing.
The descendant of Aeneas, of piety renowned,
and the ancestor of Romulus, still to arrive,
he was aware of his high duties profound,
labouring honourably for his city to thrive,
and his queen constantly did amaze,
his brilliant wife always to adore,
exalting her glory, so often to praise,
her unrivaled eyes inspiring him to soar.

But the King, leading his people brave,
was not prepared for what would befall,
for the sudden calamity ominously grave,
which would always so painfully appall.
With illness, his cherished queen soon fell,
aghast to witness her last breath,
with her vile disease unable to dispel,
stunned by the injustice of her death.

And so Tiberinus for years did weep,
overwhelmed by the excruciating pain,
flooded by the unrelenting sorrow deep,
his royal obligations now only vain,
as that desert took its dreadful place
in his aching core, without any relief,
always that ceaseless agony to face,
enslaved to the chains of his fated grief.
Bombarded by the misery without end,
a constant sword pierced his side,

his anguished soul unable to mend,
as his very existence he did deride.
The King lamented to the gods above,
questioning the tears of this tragic land,
the loss of his gloriously wondrous love,
with the torture impossible to withstand.
Nostalgic for that time when he did soar,
his unbearable days he did detest,
the prison of his existence to abhor,
so weary of life's useless quest.

So grieving Tiberinus in his torment,
fighting furiously that endless fire,
to the river bearing his name went,
exhausted by his ruinous state dire,
and in that lonely condition too weak,
under those waters he then did drown,
with his swift escape to finally seek,
as he left in mourning the entire town.

Her Smile

When she smiled, all was clear,
with those miraculous eyes of light,
as I was free of all that prior fear,
lifted to the splendor of cosmic height,
in inspired jubilation as I did fly,
her radiance triumphantly profound,
joining those chariots in the higher sky,
as harmonious trumpets did resound,
and all the stunning galaxies did beam,
with that joyful understanding to find,
as such blissful marvels did teem,
with that new serenity of mind.

In Milan

Two residents of old Milan did converse,
in a deep exchange as they did immerse.
"I've witnessed so much war and pain,
with such excessive struggle as we work,
with all the battles on this Lombard plain,
and many falling to illness which does lurk.
As the ambitious Visconti now lead,
our city struggles for a secure place,
humanity always voracious in its greed,
as this arduous climb we continue to face,
as the cities of Italy seem constantly at war,
with Venice and Florence to always compete,
with these perilous disputes to truly deplore,
as the call of Mars we're forced to greet.
Then there's the threat of French power,
as surely their aspirations will grow,
aiming to expand as a menacing tower,
anticipating now more blood to flow.

So with all this recurring pain and death,
I've come now God's existence to doubt,
seeing a child in agony take his last breath,
no longer pious as in my youth strong,
no longer sincerely dutiful nor devout,
as I question through empty nights long.
And without God, life clearly does lack
meaningful purpose, useless in its way,
while the sorrow continues to attack,
considering the end now in my dismay."

"I'm concerned about your sinking decline,
sympathetic to this decaying despair,

as you no longer trust in the Divine,
a wayward bird wandering through the air.
Thus I must take you to an acquaintance old,
a reclusive man I have known for years,
who hopefully can assist through your cold,
and alleviate all your aching tears,
as he lives closer to the mighty Alps high,
crucial to meet while this life you decry."

So the two men proceeded on their way,
heading north with their urgent sense,
travelling boldly now on this day,
battling through all their angst intense,
eventually reaching the recluse meek,
searching for some solace higher,
as sustaining wisdom they did seek,
looking to subdue all their alarm dire.

They were welcomed as they did greet,
gracious then for the opportunity to meet.
"What brings you now to my home here,
fellow pilgrims, my friends dear?
With several worries as you stir,
I see that you have come with dread;
but how did that leg wound occur,
noticing your pain now as you tread?"

To the man with the crisis he did turn,
sensing all the anguish which did burn,
and immediately noticed his laboured stride,
his injured leg from old combat which he eyed.
Then approaching with his grace to astound,
with mere touch the leg he did fully mend

in a matter of only seconds, truly profound,
as swiftly then both visitors this did send
into a dazed state of such long surprise,
with rejuvenation in their center grand,
with deep trust to keep in this land,
as they were inspired with their new eyes.

The Ego

The ruthless ego continues to enslave,
with its vicious flood of unmet desire,
trapped in this raging storm grave,
always in a battle with this inner fire.
Truly impossible to ever satisfy
its voracious appetite, insatiably grand,
this gluttonous ego which I decry
leaves me in a desert of endless sand,
as the aspirations never cease,
with dissatisfaction always profound,
unable its demands to ever appease,
to this ravenous creature now bound.
While I'm ravaged in my painful core,
I recognize the need now to transcend
these relentless chains I so deplore,
striving with my fortitude to ascend,
voyaging beyond this woeful hole
to my actual nature, deeper to find,
to reach the bliss of my eternal soul,
beyond the torment of my mind,
to arrive in those pastures green,
to finally conquer ignorance blind,
rediscovering that peace serene,
the illusive ego no longer to bind.

The Ant Hill

Observing an ant hill on a boyhood day,
I recall that dread when I did realize
that the ants seemed like us in our way,
as we face the unknown with painful cries.
They were scurrying on the harsh soil,
immersed in their meager world small,
busy with all their vain and trivial toil,
watching curiously as it did appall,
a tiny species insignificant to sense
in the vastness of the cosmos immense.
And I was filled with such lonely fear,
as they were working away so fast,
so vulnerable to death always near,
their humble colony not destined to last,
and yet no one would know nor care,
as I was engulfed by sorrow profound,
and the cold emptiness did ensnare,
as I fell in anguish to the ground.

In the North

Tired of this bleak land north,
where the snowfall shall never end,
I continue now to wander forth,
my condition impossible to mend
in this wretched tundra, barren and cold,
this desolation where nothing can grow,
struggling to maintain my hopes bold,
with my tears continuing to flow.
Despising this frozen waste of despair,
where spring shall never arrive,
deep emptiness pervades the air,
with never any satisfying joy to derive,
and unforgiving Nature doesn't care
in this constant struggle to survive,
where survival lacks a meaning great,
only bewildered by this dreadful fate.
So I continue to languish, so weak,
in this ravaging agony as I reel,
while so distant is that precious peak,
while all these wounds never heal,
still attacked by this blizzard of wrath,
all this snow continuing to pound,
losing that mighty youthful path,
always lonely without any sound,
and too old is my battered coat,
with never any warmth to be found,
with the obscured Sun only remote,
as I fall miserably to the ground.

Alexander in India

When proud Alexander the Great
finally distant India did reach,
with his men in their weary state,
with his ambitions never to breach,
he met this serene elder of age,
who intrigued him with his ways,
questioned by this bold sage,
who quickly left him in a daze.

"But I must continue and advance,
always voracious for more land,
to the world's end as I aspire,
always needing more in my trance,
and never satisfied as I expand,
looking to appease my inner fire.
Past the next great river ahead,
I must enlarge my dear empire,
with all my aspirations to be fed,
greater than valiant Achilles past,
as posterity will always admire
my cherished domain vast."

"But why do you always chase
this transient power and fame,
always trapped in this race,
travelling to remote lands far,
towards fleeting glory your aim,
when eternal bliss you already are?
Of your true nature you're not aware,
always with your hungry ego caught,
the painful chain of ambition to bear,
in this endless war to be fought,

and yet the greatest battle to wage
is actually with the ego to subdue,
to be liberated from that cage,
with deepest knowledge to pursue.
And that lasting, clear joy to seek,
conquering all the illusory mist,
is greater than any earthly peak,
a boundless ocean always to exist."

In the Desert

Thrown into this desert of dismay,
always plagued by my weary mind,
under tyrannical sorrow's sway,
crucial hope I struggle to find,
as I decay in this horrid heat,
facing this torturous unknown,
mournful in this insignificant seat,
walking in this desolate land alone.
But yearning still for that prior glow,
I long to flee all this lonely sand,
towards the cherished waters to flow,
striving to keep my mission grand.

To be Free

As I continue in agony to weep
in this darkness with weary eyes,
sinking in this vicious void deep,
in this harsh land I now realize
that towards liberation I must steer,
past the torment of this bleak plain,
towards the everlasting light dear,
longing to release each aching chain,
with the desire to truly soar unbound,
as the cherished birds in their height,
to escape this miserable ground
and finally regain my prior might.
As this vile emptiness I disdain,
in the depths of this remote sea,
out of this prison of piercing pain
my core now yearns to be free.

Momentary Glance

With only a momentary glance
upon her Beauty which did inspire,
she left me in a serene trance,
quieting the anguish of my fire,
as the Transcendent she did bring
with those grand euphoric eyes,
hearing celebrating spirits sing,
swiftly lifted into the higher skies.
Though painfully I could not be
joined with her in this grueling life,
her glory was boundless as the sea,
rescuing my ship from all the strife,
as I shall always exalt and praise
the wonder of her emanating light,
recalling again that jubilant daze,
when I was taken to that height,
when Beauty I did briefly understand,
the way it inspires the core to align,
manifesting its radiance in this land,
illuminating our path to the Divine,
as it guides on the great climb long,
through all this arduous snow,
rejuvenating with energies strong,
and sustaining with its ardent glow,
leading us to that majestic peak,
where Love does eternally flow,
to that glory which we seek,
with true bliss to finally know.

In this Cave

In this vile cave I can never appease
my inner chasm, always so intense,
with all the agony never to cease,
always left with this gloomy sense,
plagued by the constant hole to decry,
with no remedy for this pain innate,
and nothing satisfying in this land dry,
so distressed by this human state.
Yet I know that I am truly meant
to be free of this misty and lonely cave,
as I must strive for my crucial ascent,
fortified with my renewed efforts brave,
towards that beaming castle to arrive,
no longer in my weariness to languish,
as our radiance will always thrive,
with the unknown to finally vanquish,
towards the Sun with the birds high,
journeying deeper as I long to discern,
past this old prison as I must fly
to the glorious One to finally return.

Towards the Infinite

There is never contentment complete
in this life where our ambitions burn,
as this emptiness we always meet,
as the restlessness long does churn
amidst all the sorrow of this plane,
always struggling for more to secure
while our aspiring souls still maintain
that deepest longing for vision pure.
We can only be fulfilled by the Divine,
by the Infinite, our most crucial desire,
aspiring through our suffering to align
to reach that majestic splendor higher;
though it is an arduous ascent long,
it is a meaningful trek as we strive,
through the winters remaining strong,
back to our cherished home to arrive.

On the Path

Voyaging alone on my path,
struggling through this barren land,
I must endure this sorrow's wrath,
while maintaining my focus grand,
and I'm strengthened now by the trust
that liberation is possible to secure,
meant for immortal awareness august,
beyond this agony which does stir,
as we are truly more than fleeting dust,
always tied with that which did manifest
this harmonious cosmos, as I must
cultivate new fortitude on this quest,
as it is the innate capacity of each
to develop the ultimate sight high,
that complete knowledge to reach,
towards that joy to finally fly.

With resilience on this long road,
I long to be free of all the pain,
to finally release this heavy load,
conquering desires and every stain.
With new strength which does teem,
with a devoted and courageous voice,
I yearn for the Godhead Supreme,
the glory of the Infinite as I rejoice,
to the One which does transcend,
striving for that dear peak as I grow,
to unite with Brahman as I ascend,
with Eternal bliss to truly know.

Homesick

I'm deeply homesick for my land,
for those serene fields I adore,
with that constant jubilation grand,
where in that joy I once did soar.
And I long once again to stand
amidst that wonder, free of war,
to flee this empty desert sand,
and embrace that loving shore.

The Monk

Near glorious peaks to behold,
I was caught in this long fight,
as we struggled our position to hold
against relentless invaders of might,
as the combat provoked such dread,
with widespread panic just to survive,
and yet our dutiful strength did spread,
defending with valor as we did strive.

Eventually of that battle I was free,
and I walked pensively further ahead,
as this humble monastery I did see,
towards this mountain as I did tread;
meeting this generous monk inside,
he already knew that I would appear,
welcoming me after my tired stride,
providing this cherished insight dear,
conversing with me as an old friend,
while my deep curiosity did increase,
as he then aspired to finally mend
my battered core, offering peace.

"You have suffered through much pain,
through much anguish and despair,
which inspires you now to commence
to move beyond this limited plane,
to purify and reach the sacred air,
devoting all your labour to the Divine,
as already that glory you sense,
thinking past the common line.
As the individual life swiftly flies,
focus not on the temporary and brief,

but on the Eternal, past even the skies,
even while struggling with your grief,
as you progress to crucially realize
that we are all part of God vast,
meant over your aching abyss to rise,
journeying past the stubborn veil,
all united with Brahman to last,
as to deep knowing you must sail.

Do not identify with your body and mind,
with all that tormenting emotional dismay,
but turn to your deepest core to find
that it is equal to Brahman in its way,
as you must strive for moksha, to be free,
towards that celestial bliss without end,
finally your true nature to joyously see,
one with the Infinite which does transcend.
Everything is really the one Absolute high,
meant to ascend this relative state,
after all our advancing lives as we fly,
finally to be free of all painful weight.
And you are already in union to revere,
only a matter of realization to attain,
towards liberating knowledge to steer,
vanquishing all ignorance, that stain,
no longer to mourn with that hole,
as you aspire towards that vision clear,
as direct experience must be your goal,
conquering all suffering and fear.

So beyond your tempestuous mind,
no longer attached to emotion dire,

free of the old desires which bind,
concentrating with calmness higher,
that lasting fountain you must know,
finally surmounting all your despair,
where pristine waters always flow,
with ultimate consciousness aware."

Eternity Triumphant

There was that perilous time
when the uncertainty did torment,
unsure of the wondrous sublime,
with the vast unknown to lament,
when in my doubts I then did steer,
distressed by death, oblivion's chance,
overwhelmed by such aching fear,
the anguish of that piercing lance.
But now I'm assured by each sign,
as Eternity is triumphant over despair,
as I recognize the boundless Divine,
no longer with all that angst to bear.
With glimpses of that blissful light,
I strive with my devotion to ascend
to those euphoric fields to unite,
my immortal fortress to transcend;
advancing even while tears flow,
climbing with purpose on my course,
I must align with Love as I grow,
to the Absolute, the Infinite Source.

A Knight

With his aspirations to maintain,
the dutiful knight now did engage
in noble discussion, as he did explain
his circumstances to a hermit sage.
"Back in my kingdom I adore,
our growing strength to defend,
miraculously in such joy I did soar,
amazed to so suddenly ascend
upon first meeting that Lady fair,
with the wonder of her radiant eyes
and the splendor of her flowing hair,
her remarkable glory always to rise,
her form clearly of a Divine mold,
left in that daze when I did behold.
Soon I was astonished to discover
that she was the daughter of the King,
usually kept in much fortified cover,
this brilliant princess who did sing,
known for her angelic voice high,
charming the birds as they did fly.

When the King I then did address,
my Love for his daughter to reveal,
detailing my admiration in distress,
fighting my apprehension as I did reel,
my devotion he soon did understand,
and yet he would only provide her hand
upon the fulfillment of a certain condition,
sending me then on this arduous mission.
I was tasked then with securing gold
from this remote kingdom of wealth,
to prove my abilities, valiantly bold,

to advance with tenacity and stealth.
It was a demanding journey long,
with numerous doubts on the way,
inspired by my Lady and her song,
yet weary after each grueling day.
Crossing many a river and plain,
evading each guarding fort,
the gold I eventually did gain,
penetrating that foreign court.
So now I'm striving to return,
travelling back to my great home,
to unite with the princess as I yearn,
again in my childhood fields to roam."

In reply, the hermit showed concern,
reflecting now as he did discern.
"Your King does truly appear
as a cruel sovereign with his force;
you cherish his wonderful daughter dear,
and yet he sends you on this course.
He is probably another of that kind
who never satisfaction shall attain,
always plotting with his selfish mind,
occupied only by the material and vain,
likely always seeking more land,
hungry for prosperity and gold,
his precious treasury to expand,
and questing for more power to hold.
Many are much too attached here,
forgetting their origins Above,
descending further in their fear,
spiraling away from the Father's Love.

Yet as majestic Beauty we can detect,
we must strive to know the Divine,
to better appreciate and connect,
as we must aspire to finally align."

Grateful for the wisdom higher,
the knight resumed his path ahead,
filled with vigorous passion and desire,
moving faster as he now did tread.
Now close to his revered land,
and inspired by her celestial face,
he anticipated a glorious union grand,
eager to finally and jubilantly embrace.

Yet upon his return he soon did find
a fierce battle which furiously did rage,
with great fears flooding his mind,
as a rival power had chosen to wage
another massive threatening campaign,
watching his fellow knights in pain;
always another invasion to meet,
the enemy cavalry did advance,
as their frenzied charge did greet
with many a crippling lance.
The carnage appalling to see,
he summoned his energies brave,
never from his duties to flee,
and ready his kingdom to save,
as he joined the combat immense,
striving now his realm to defend,
into the heart of the struggle intense
and enveloped in that long turmoil,
as many opponents he did send
to the desolation of that soil.

Yet with that outnumbering horde,
increasingly difficult to sustain,
he was pierced by a vengeful sword,
as he fell in shock to the cold plain,
yelling in excruciating agony great,
completely bewildered by his fate.
Now he knew his death was near:
never with the princess to unite,
never her voice again to hear,
destroyed in that ruthless fight.
Yet as he lay then on the ground,
he recalled the hermit's words wise,
while all that chaos did surround,
as he turned to the glorious skies,
and deep serenity he then found,
his blissful core ready to rise.

With Apollo

I was on a weary walk for days,
as the harsh storms I did fight,
engulfed in my anguished haze,
and quickly losing all my might,
as I endured that vicious cold,
alone on that uncertain path,
struggling all my hopes to hold,
with the wind's wounding wrath.
Finally I was blessed to find
a majestic temple beaming near,
swiftly captivating my tired mind
with its glorious columns dear.
So inside the temple I then went
and radiant Apollo was there,
renewed in my joyful ascent,
so grateful in that purified air,
as Apollo so swiftly did astound,
stunned by the sight grand,
and his mighty voice did resound
after days on that barren land.

"Now the arrogant moderns vain
compel me so often to weep,
their blindness a source of pain,
as they neglect their soul deep.
In disbelief, they don't appreciate
sacred poetry, the art sublime,
humanity descending in its state,
since the serenity of that golden time.
They've forgotten that Beauty is Divine
and indicative of the highest Source,
as they no longer strive to align,

only wandering on their errant course.
And yet inspiration you have found,
as to immortal poetry you did turn,
open to the lyre's soaring sound,
devoted to this art as you yearn.
It is this Beauty which can heal
your sorrowful emptiness vast,
through suffering's grueling wheel,
with all your aspirations to last.
With your deep fortitude to maintain,
striving with that burdening weight,
even through all your grief on this plain,
continue always your mission to create."

On the Wheel

This dreaded combat fierce
never relents in its vile way,
with this agony always to pierce,
as I'm besieged each dreary day.
It seems I'm continually sent
as a weary soldier to sustain
once again this ravaging torment,
this anguished chaos and pain.
Amidst the remnants in this land,
constantly I'm forced to face
these cruel armies which expand,
with only this isolation to embrace.
So on this excruciating wheel,
these harsh years always to bear,
I long so ardently to finally heal,
to be lifted from this despair.

Miraculous Eyes

I was in that tedious wilderness dire
when she wondrously did appear,
strengthened by her Beauty higher,
and astounded by her presence near,
as her miraculous eyes did inspire,
with that majestic triumph to hear.
I was lifted in that celestial trance,
stunned in those pure waters to steer,
and reborn after that glorious glance
always to cherish her glory dear;
awed by her splendor immense,
I was emboldened to better sustain
all the recurring agony of this plain,
with this new awareness to sense,
as Beauty signals as it does show
the revered path to the Source's flow,
as a new opening it did then provide
through all the mountains and snow,
with that pinnacle to be eyed,
finally aware of the limitless glow.

The Sage of the Forest

Deep in the forests I did explore,
meditating on the profound,
with grand thoughts as I did soar,
distant from the city's sound.
And soon I was humbled to sight
a certain lake which did amaze,
and that swan of majestic white,
so illuminated by the Sun's rays.
Then emerging was a man old,
who seemed in this forest to reside,
eager to commence his address bold,
with his glorious light to provide.

"I must share my message great
with metaphysical insight to bring,
the ancient wisdom to restate,
inspired since my youth to sing.
I've contemplated for years long,
with my inner refuge to reach,
and now with harmonious song
I'm ready for many to teach.
And I'm dedicated now to strive
the bold West to crucially save,
revered Europa to finally revive
from its nihilistic chaos grave.
From their current blindness dark
I must now rescue many vain,
with recognition of their lasting spark,
with liberation from this valley's pain.
With sacred waters to renew,
many need rejuvenation to pursue
their true mission in this land,

meant to flourish once more,
with hopes and aspirations grand,
sensing within their true core.
There is a critical need to return
to the glory of the underlying Divine,
to that for which we all yearn,
with the perennial wisdom to align.
Though some resistance I will face,
each soul is really aspiring to mend,
as the Infinite many will embrace,
with Love triumphant, as we ascend."

To Unite

Even as the anguish does flow,
I must continue always to endure,
with that Kingdom to truly know,
striving to reach my nature pure.
Yearning to be free of the wheel,
I must reach that wonder innate,
with those endless waters to heal,
past these wounds of aching weight.
Through all the sorrow and pain,
through my long struggle intense,
I must labour to better sustain,
with greater Beauty now to sense,
with courage as I must maintain
my crucial and cherished quest,
even through this arduous plain,
even as agony continues to test.
As the Father I always revere,
in this long pursuit I must persist,
now transcending all my fear,
to that joy beyond the mist.
Though in this land I often weep,
I must endeavor now to rise,
journeying to my core deep,
to ascend to the Highest skies,
past all this suffering which I face,
as I long for that momentous flight,
finally with that lasting embrace,
towards the Infinite to unite.